CONTENTS

FROM THE EDITOR

Leigh Steinberg is the most well-known sports agent in the world, having represented over 300 professional athletes. He is also the real-life inspiration for the move, *Jerry Maguire*. He is also a philanthropist and a bestselling author.

Never one to rest on his laurels, Leigh is now embarking on yet another venture, one that will touch even more lives—The Steinberg Sports Academy.

The Steinberg Sports Academy is a private high school that combines high-level academics with sports. But this isn't just another sports-focused school. Students will receive a rigorous education and will graduate with a two-year college degree.

Some students will go on to play professional sports, others will become involved in sports-related careers, but all of them will learn leadership skills, perseverance, and discipline.

This issue focuses on those involved in the Steinberg Sports Academy, including those who participated in their inaugural football camp that took place in Mesa, AZ on April 1 at the Legacy Sports Complex, the site of the academy's first physical location.

PIVOT Magazine

Founder and President
Jason Miller
jason@strategicadvisorboard.com

Editor-in-Chief
Chris O'Byrne
chris@jetlaunch.net

Design
JETLAUNCH.net

Advertising
Chris O'Byrne
chris@jetlaunch.net

Webmaster
Joel Phillips
joel@proshark.com

Editor
Laura West
laura@jetlaunch.net

Cover Design
Debbie O'Byrne

FROM THE DESK OF THE PRESIDENT

JASON MILLER

Recently, I had the opportunity to attend the inaugural sports camp hosted by the Steinberg Sports Academy. We brought four exceptional NFL clients to the camp, where they made a significant impact. This event marked the kickoff for the Steinberg Sports Academy, and we all felt honored to be a part of it. We were thrilled to participate and contribute to the academy's bigger picture.

My involvement with the academy began almost a year ago. I often tell people that connections can lead to unexpected opportunities, so focusing on them is essential. I have made connections in my business career that led to fruitful outcomes years later. One such relationship was with Dr. Julie Ducharme. Over a year ago, she told me about the Steinberg Sports Academy, which was still in its infancy.

Dr. Ducharme wanted to organize an NFL football camp, and as we had four NFL clients, I suggested bringing them to participate in the first camp. She was excited about the idea and did an outstanding job organizing the event alongside Coach Stone. We brought the influence of our NFL clients to the camp, but it all started with a simple conversation over a year ago. This experience underscores the importance of always having those conversations because you never know where they may lead.

I was recently appointed as one of the board of directors for the Steinberg Sports Academy, which I consider an absolute honor. I am now part of a diverse group of accomplished individuals, including former athletes and business giants in their respective industries, all working together to shape the future of this fantastic academy.

Being a board member is a significant responsibility, and I do not take it lightly. My input, along with that of the other board members, will directly influence the direction and success of the academy. Given the importance and scope of this academy, it's a substantial responsibility. Providing input and collaborating with such a remarkable group of individuals on the board is both humbling and awe-inspiring.

From a business point of view, the Steinberg Sports Academy's (SSA) success relies heavily on how the business side supports the growth and development of youth. Sponsorships and fundraising will play a crucial role in the Academy's success.

As parents of young children, we recognize that today's world demands a balanced approach combining academic education and developing life skills. Learning teamwork, handling pressure, and building resiliency are essential components of a well-rounded education for future business owners and leaders.

Business and academics go hand in hand, as they support and complement each other. We must utilize the business side of the Academy to foster the growth of our youth and introduce sports dynamics into their lives. As the saying goes, "An idle mind creates trouble." Many children who lack positive outlets for their energy find themselves in trouble.

An all-in-one academy that seamlessly integrates sports and academics can be a powerful tool. By keeping young people engaged and teaching them leadership skills, alongside other essential life lessons through sports, we can significantly impact their lives and futures.

I believe it's crucial for the academy to teach students about business. If we look back in history, we were once cavemen, using stones to make fire and hunting for our food. We were entrepreneurs; there were no grocery stores, and our survival depended on our resourcefulness.

Integrating this entrepreneurial mentality into the academy's curriculum is vital. It provides students with additional choices, options, and skills to utilize in their lives. One can never have too many options or learn too much. Lifelong learning is essential for personal growth. Regardless of age, there is always something new to discover.

The day we stop learning is the day we cease to grow.

Continuing to grow is essential for most people, and providing options in business education enables the development of leadership skills, money management, and financial decision-making. Business and entrepreneurship is one of the least discussed topics in our school systems. Students should be educated on finances, running a business, and other career options.

Just as some students choose to join the military, others may want to explore various fields such as sports, business, medicine, law, and more. By offering specific, relevant information and options in schools, we can help students expand their minds and consider different career paths.

Instead of focusing solely on traditional subjects that may never be used again, we should allow students to make informed choices during their formative years. This approach will better prepare them for their futures, no matter what path they choose.

What would make me want to send my own children to the Steinberg Sports Academy is its dynamic approach that offers more than what traditional high schools provide. Of course, I'm not dismissing conventional high schools, but let me give you an example.

When my son was in kindergarten, he scored a bit lower on tests than his peers. However, when you observe him, you can see how intuitive he is and how much he has learned outside of school. Tests don't always accurately reflect a person's actual skills.

For instance, my wife struggled with math in high school, yet she has two master's degrees and is a certified project manager.

Some people are good test takers, while others are not. I would want to send my own children to the academy because it offers a blend of education and sports. Additionally, it provides a shortcut to college, allowing students to complete their bachelor's degrees in just two extra years. That's a significant advantage if they choose to pursue it.

I have an MBA, but I would say it has contributed very little to my business acumen. I believe more in the school of hard knocks when it comes to business—learning as you go and doing as you learn because that's what life is all about. School can only teach so much.

At some point, you have to go out and learn from real-life experiences, getting knocked down and figuring things out. We all had to do that, and it will never go away. However, giving someone the tools that the Steinberg Sports Academy provides can offer our youth a better head start compared to an average public school.

Part of my job as a board member is to focus on scaling the academy from a business perspective. This involves obtaining proper funding and finding the right sponsors to expand across the United States and overseas. Many countries have already expressed interest in building an academy.

It's crucial to strike a delicate balance in pacing budgets, growth, and other aspects of the academies to ensure scalability. This way, we can break ground in one state after another. However, since it's a private school, private funding will play a significant role, so we must be cautious and avoid overextending ourselves.

We need to be careful not to let our ambitions outpace our resources. It's essential to plan budgets meticulously, as businesses like this can falter quickly if not managed correctly. Establishing a 16-acre campus requires substantial funding, staff, and resources—no small feat.

My strength as a board member lies in guiding and helping the academy navigate this process, which is why they brought me onto the board in the first place.

Another unique and remarkable aspect of SSA is that it's not just about the kids but also the parents. The academy aims to integrate parents more effectively into the educational system than what we often see in public schools. As a parent with kids in the public system, I can attest that we're not as involved as we could be.

SSA strives to create a better dynamic by involving parents in both the academic and sports sides of their children's lives. This approach allows parents to feel more connected to their kids' learning and doing, fostering a well-rounded family dynamic inside and outside the home. I believe anything that positively affects home life is a huge win.

Embarking on this incredible journey alongside Leigh Steinberg, Ray Powers, and other influential figures in sports and business will be an exciting experience for me.

LEIGH STEINBERG

The Steinberg Sports Academy's inspiration originated from our education system's shortcomings. As the son of a high school principal who was once a teacher and then a vice principal, education has always been close to my heart.

Steinberg Sports hosts sports career conferences in our other ventures, so creating a specialized high school seemed like a natural progression. Our primary goal is to ensure that athletes who attend our academy possess a strong foundation in math, science, and other essential skills to be competitive in today's job market.

However, the overarching concept addresses the immense interest among young people worldwide in pursuing careers in the sports industry. These careers could range from working for a team, franchise, league, conference, or university athletic department to working with players' associations.

Other opportunities include sports marketing, branding, sports media (both on-air and support roles), sports writing, and facilities management. Our curriculum emphasizes these subjects, providing students with specialized training in their areas of interest.

The academy caters to athletes and non-athletes, those who may not necessarily have a future as professional athletes. Predicting which students will pursue sports as a career can be challenging. Regardless, they may still have a passion for sports, and our goal is to bridge that gap.

We aim to provide consistent skill training for young kids, similar to what we conducted in Mesa, AZ at our football camp. We will continue to offer these programs at regular intervals.

The ultimate goal is to create a new educational model focused on sports, which will also lead to broader opportunities. Our practice emphasizes the concept of role modeling. We strive to teach athletes and young professionals how to retrace their roots, engage with high school, collegiate, and professional communities, and make a positive impact.

For instance, we established the Sporting Green Alliance to introduce sustainable technology to sports facilities, such as wind, solar, recycling, and water conservation. This reduces carbon emissions and energy costs, transforming these spaces into educational platforms where fans can learn about solar panels and other green technology and consider implementing them in their own homes.

By placing sports at the forefront, we can demonstrate how athletes can create anti-bullying programs and champion causes like preventing domestic violence. This approach inspires change in young people more effectively than a thousand authority figures ever could. Through sports, we can address issues like domestic violence, sex trafficking, bullying, racism, and more.

We can also teach networking skills, demonstrating how to use public events to build relationships that will benefit them in future careers. While the kids we will be working with may be young, older athletes can learn how to approach someone, engage in a meaningful five-minute conversation, and establish connections to help them in their careers.

The Steinberg Sports Academy addresses many parents' dissatisfaction with the current state of education, which often neglects to teach core skills and fails to adequately prepare students for careers. We believe classic truths should be emphasized, and this approach has a market. On the other hand, sports have become increasingly influential, with new stadiums, jumbo scoreboards, enhanced television contracts, merchandising, and gambling, among other things.

In the past, I had formed a company called Athlete Direct, which users accessed through AOL. It allowed athletes to share their weekly diaries, discuss their charities, and sell merchandise directly to fans. We initially invested $100,000 in the venture and later sold our share for $25 million.

Today, some young people will become entrepreneurs, creating new websites, engaging with new sports, or identifying unfulfilled niches. There are also breakthroughs in biomedicine that relate to two key areas. The first is finding modalities that can enhance focus, hand-eye coordination, and endurance during the final moments of a game. The second is helping players recover more quickly from injuries, particularly when their backup, under a salary cap system, is less talented.

Addressing the issue of concussions is also essential. As potential treatment methods, we have discovered hyperbaric oxygen, stem cells, red and blue light infusions, NanoVi, and various cognitive processes can be very helpful. Our students will be involved with these innovative healing modalities, which seventeen NFL teams have already adopted to enhance performance. Our goal is for our students to be at the forefront of the massive transformation occurring in preventative and rehabilitative medicine that actually improves performance.

We have set ambitious goals, such as teaching students specific skills to assist them in college and their future careers. For instance, students might attend law school or study sports marketing and learn the basic principles of their chosen field. However, many educational institutions do not teach essential skills like networking and personal branding.

Also, understanding another person's perspective is vital. This involves empathizing with their fears, anxieties, hopes, and dreams and seeing the world through their eyes. This skill is not often taught, but it can help people connect with others and develop a deeper understanding of their priorities, such as faith, long-term economic security, family matters, and personal aspirations.

Developing this ability to understand others' perspectives can aid in recruitment or sales, which are often integral to various careers. It can also enhance negotiation skills and help with personal branding and marketing. While we aim to teach these specific skill sets, we also strive to cultivate high-character young people with the mission and vision to create a better world.

My father instilled in me two core values: the importance of relationships, especially within the family, and the drive to make a meaningful difference in the lives of those who cannot help themselves. These values underpin the new skills we aim to impart to our students. If successful, we hope to inspire a trend of positive change.

We have planned numerous unique opportunities for our students, such as negotiation exercises. In previous iterations, we have invited the head of Fox Sports to discuss television contracts and general managers from professional sports teams to share insights. We have also organized stadium tours to examine marketing strategies.

Our curriculum also includes teaching damage control. For instance, we assign students a "troubled" athlete and task them with creating press releases or statements while engaging with real reporters. We can collaborate with local sports franchises in football, baseball, basketball, and hockey for interactive learning experiences. Additionally, we will cover emerging fields like e-sports, inviting industry professionals to discuss their perspectives on the sport, marketing, and branding.

We will also address the growing influence of name, image, and likeness (NILs) on college campuses, where athletes can now hire marketing agents. Our focus is on providing a well-rounded education that empowers students to use their primary profession for the greater good. Students will receive practical skills training in areas such as networking, negotiation, sales, and even sports writing.

Our goal is to create a vibrant, exciting campus with strong educational credentials and the creativity necessary to meet the demands of the modern market.

NONPROFIT OF THE MONTH THE SYNERGY LEARNING INSTITUTE

The Synergy Learning Institute was built to help veterans transitioning from the rigors of military life to the much more unstructured civilian life. With programs like "Combat Boots to High Heels," SLI has much to teach and willing, eager minds to grow and overachieve, but not without bumps and bruises.

Join us as Will Black, CEO of Sharing the Credit, interviews Dr. Julie Ducharme, who in addition to running four successful businesses, is also the Chief Academic Officer for the Steinberg School of Sports.

Will: Julie, you are a serial entrepreneur. I've seen what you do and know the honor you heap on our military. But launching and successfully running Synergy Learning Institute was no small feat. How? Why? Do you just enjoy punishment?

Dr. Julie: I was a college dean, and the faculty kept telling me we needed programs to help vets transition to civilian life. It was ears-to-the-ground good intel, but I could not get the college to see its value. It's the classic people telling you what's needed scenario. They wouldn't listen, so I launched my own college, one where vets could take the programs at no cost.

Will: Where did that come from? How did you find that kind of inner mettle?

Dr. Julie: My legacy to my children comes from my mother, who passed about ten years ago. Suffering from a disease and having to ride a cart did not keep her from giving to the homeless, knitting caps for cancer patients, raising money for underprivileged kids who couldn't afford to go to prom, and raising money for kids who couldn't afford registration fees. I promised her I'd keep that torch going. The summer after her death, our first automotive program for vets launched with my father's help. Even my children are helping to keep that going.

Will: Promise kept! That is inspiring. Also, I feel a little lazy now. I have to ask... These things are never easy. This is no primrose path. So tell me about the bumps.

Dr. Julie: Building means heartache, too. A few years ago, my partners were sent to opposite ends of the planet. It got to where they could not maintain the workload. That was a gut punch. I thought sometimes I was crazy to launch what we did, but if I could go back to my much younger self, playing pro volleyball, I'd tell her, as crazy as it sounds, we would someday do this huge thing, it would work, and it would keep going. But here's the WHY. Why I keep going forward is that I have had veterans say they were suicidal, and this turned it around for them. To the outsider, that might sound wonderful and like a significant burden at the same time. It's not a burden. It's rocket fuel!

Will: Julie, you know Leigh Steinberg is on the cover this month. After all, it was you who introduced us to him. How did you come to get in front of Steinberg in the first place?

Dr. Julie: I have been blessed to have some fantastic partners, and Ray Powers is among them. When he told me about the school he was building out and that he had Leigh's support, I told him I was in! I have been in academia for twenty-three years and have seen that not all educational changes were good. We saw that with COVID. Changing education and kids' lives by creating better-educated leaders for the future was all I needed to know.

Will: Here's a genie-in-a-bottle scenario for the Institute. What's your wish?

Dr. Julie: Funding, Will. Funding, funding, funding. We don't just educate and help people jump to better and more prosperous lives; we sometimes save them from death. Hope does that. Education gives hope to these men and women who keep us safe.

Will: You do a lot. I've seen you at work. As silly as it is, were they to make a movie about you building the Synergy Learning Institute, what would your theme song be?

Dr. Julie: Wonder Woman's theme! I love her moral ethics and giving heart.

You can see more about the institute here: https://synergylearninginstitute.org/

You can support veterans' classes and the community if you have a business. Click below or use the QR code, and we'll show you how to give to them in pre-tax dollars.

Yes, I'd like my business to help vets get a good education.

SCAN ME

RAY POWERS

I grew up in an orphanage until the age of six and was then adopted by parents who couldn't have children but dedicated their lives to disadvantaged children. Over the years, they took in over one hundred of us as foster or adopted children. Of course, we all had problems due to the experiences of our first years of life. But aside from being grateful for their human kindness, I and many of my "brothers and sisters" learned that life isn't predetermined and that we can achieve goals we set out to accomplish, even when circumstances seem unfavorable.

I guess I'm a serial entrepreneur and innovator who always believes there are better ways to achieve goals and create mutual benefits. As a product of the traditional public school system and an advocate of education as the key to success, I recognize the extraordinary opportunities an innovative path to excellence in education provides. Examples of excellence include the integration of higher-order thinking even before entering high school, the practical application of academic theory rather than the traditional parametric perspective, and the mentoring and ongoing guidance students receive as key to achieving their goals. Other benefits offered by these approaches include the individual, socioeconomic, and cultural values that excellence in education brings.

At AT&T, I was tasked with setting up the first project management office. Although they had developed great projects, there was no formal way to manage them. When I created this group, I found that the people I was hiring didn't have the necessary skills for the job.

There was no efficient way to train them in leadership, project management discipline, entrepreneurship, and other essential qualities for a successful project manager or leader. To solve this problem, I worked with several universities to develop a master's degree program in technology management (for lack of a better term).

This endeavor proved to be quite successful and unexpectedly led me into academia. Due to the popularity of the master's program, I taught as an adjunct and gradually became more involved in academic activities.

Eventually, I was invited to join the University of Arizona Global Campus, where I became a professor and dean of the Forbes School of Business. One of my responsibilities was to act as a liaison to Forbes. So I approached Steve Forbes and asked him if he'd be willing to serve on an advisory board and advise us.

In the academic world, it can be easy to focus too much on concepts and theories and lose sight of their applicability in practice. Steve Forbes, a brilliant and down-to-earth individual, was just the person to provide us with valuable insight. He always had insightful answers at the ready and was responsive in every conversation.

When Steve Forbes joined the board I chaired, it was much easier to attract other high-profile individuals. This created a strong advisory board that could better ensure that our academic programs were aligned with the practical needs of the world.

We attracted an impressive group of individuals to the advisory board, including Rich Karlgaard, the publisher of Parks Magazine, and Ken Fisher of Fisher Investments. Ken, a billionaire who isn't swayed by the opinions of others, openly shared his experiences and thoughts, although this isn't the place to report on them.

The seventeen-member panel was a mix of academic experts and businesspeople, emphasizing the latter. The goal was to gain insight into the value of education and what the business community expects from our graduates. In addition, we wanted to understand how well we were preparing them for the real world.

It quickly became apparent that our educational program fell short. Our students excelled in academic theory, but the question was how they'd perform in operational practice.

The question of how to improve our educational offerings repeatedly emerged within the college. Most universities face similar challenges, and in their defense, there are certain limits to developing new programs, courses, or degrees. For those unfamiliar with academia, the process can be pretty restrictive.

To introduce new programs, universities must apply to the Department of Education and undergo accreditation. While there are several accrediting bodies, it was the Western Association in this case. Both processes can take months, if not years. In addition, each state has its own accreditation requirements for teaching.

In addition to external regulations, internal guidelines exist, as found in any corporate structure. In the case of higher education institutions, these include the faculty senate and administration, which can further complicate the introduction of new programs and courses.

Developing a new technology degree program can be a lengthy process. By the time it's offered to students, and they complete it to enter the business world, the content may already be outdated. As a business and higher education advocate, I've concluded that we need a different approach to better prepare students for the workforce.

One way to do this is to introduce real-world degrees and certificates that provide the skills needed for success in the business world. These could be offered in addition to, or as supplements to, academic degrees. In our culture, there is often a lot of emphasis on earning an advanced degree to succeed, but degrees alone may not fully prepare you for a business career.

Learning from experience, mistakes, and mentors can be essential to career success. This isn't a criticism of the academic community, but finding different ways to improve the educational process is important. However, like most universities, they aren't open to change.

When I realized I should put my convictions into action, I decided to start a company called Envisage Global. The company works with universities to ensure academic quality and the right approach while collaborating with industry, curriculum development organizations, and other entities to offer non-degree certificates that target specific skills.

To understand the context, it's important to know how we arrived at this solution. Of course, no person can do everything well, but if we bring together a group of experts, we can enhance success.

Envisage Global forms strategic alliances with various organizations that need or offer curriculum development. We help market their programs, guide them through an evaluation process, and provide additional support.

One of my strategic partners was an organization that focuses on education in the world of sports. It addresses aspects such as athlete health, leadership skills, and other elements relevant to all sports, with a focus on sports. Working with this partner led to discussions about improving the educational process.

While I'm not necessarily critical of the educational community, there is undoubtedly room for improvement. As a professor, I've found that even graduate students have difficulty thinking critically and incorporating higher-order thinking into discussions, often exhibiting bias and telling instructors what they think they want to hear without substantiating their claims.

This situation raises concerns about our country's future and our educational system's effectiveness. If our educational process falls behind, it could have severe implications for the progress and well-being of our country.

Considering the future of my children, grandchildren, community, and all stakeholders, we felt a better solution was possible. Of course, getting to the root of the problem is complex, but one way to address it was to introduce higher-order thinking as early as the ninth grade in high school. We incorporate this in the Steinberg Sports Academy.

That way, high school students can get their basic education while beginning to understand the intricacies of success. For example, success doesn't necessarily mean becoming the CEO of a company. You can be a leader and excel in any job if you apply the right traits and use the proper discipline and tools to make the best contribution.

In collaboration with several universities, we have developed a dual curriculum for students that addresses these needs.

Our approach aims for students to graduate from high school with a diploma and a two-year college degree, depending on state regulations. We accomplish this by having university partners assess our courses, incorporating higher-order thinking, and assigning appropriate tasks that promote these skills instead of merely assigning busywork.

One of our partners, a group within the University of California system, has a network of 350 prominent CEOs who offer internships to high school students. These internships provide real work experience with specific goals and criteria that enhance learning. We're careful not to overwhelm students but also know that many students in public high schools are under-challenged.

The emphasis is on high academic standards coupled with the opportunity to excel in sports. Although Leigh Steinberg's name is a significant marketing factor, the program isn't just about sports. Those who want to become sports stars have the resources and connections to realize their ambitions, but the program aims to provide well-rounded opportunities for growth and development.

In sports, there are numerous opportunities beyond the role of a top athlete. For example, one can pursue a career as a sports director, health care provider, broadcaster, agent, and more. Leigh teaches sports agencies and shares his extensive contact list, which provides valuable resources for students.

Our startup has advantages over traditional businesses because we have a wealth of connections and expertise from the beginning. For example, we plan to assemble an advisory board with academic and athletic expertise. This board will include university presidents who provide academic credibility and high-profile sports figures, giving us a strong foundation that goes beyond the typical high school coaching experience.

We have carefully and cautiously developed our school in recent years while maintaining high standards. We aim to serve the entire community, not just an elite group. This is a challenge because we want to provide a well-rounded experience for all students.

Our competitors typically focus on athletic opportunities without rigorous academic requirements or offer no athletic opportunities. Our approach provides both a dual degree program for students who want high-level experience and a pathway for those who need time to develop academically or athletically. We want to give students the opportunity to improve, regardless of their current abilities.

The school concept is designed to accommodate students at different levels while striving for elite goals. We want to support students already performing well and those who aspire to higher goals. I hope this statement helps clarify the origins and intentions of our school.

Our current partnership with Legacy Sports and the Bell Bank Park facility has been beneficial. This fantastic facility is state of the art throughout. It would have been difficult to build such a facility as a private school, so we partnered with Legacy Sports to get a top-notch facility while maintaining our educational philosophy.

The complex is in financial trouble due to COVID-19, supply chain problems, and other factors. In addition, they have defaulted on their bonds, likely resulting in bondholders taking a loss. Nevertheless, we wanted to minimize our risk and avoid being burdened by the complex's financial problems.

We had planned to purchase a contiguous parcel of 320 acres to facilitate student access. However, due to the financial situation, we had to reconsider. Fortunately, the landowner will get some of the land back and has agreed to give us 15 acres. Initially, we thought we needed 10 acres, but this arrangement should work well for our needs.

We're also working with Park University, which has agreed to build a dormitory on our campus that we can rent. This provides us with a revenue stream to offset costs, and we can use their faculty and professors to teach some of our high school classes. So the strategic alliance provides mutual value and benefit to both institutions.

The property owner has assigned us a site near the entrance to the park, which gives us a lot of exposure. In addition, it's across the street from a large shopping center and three hotels currently under construction. With these facilities, we can accommodate the parents of boarding students and offer additional resources. A residential development is also planned nearby, which adds to the appeal of our location.

Our relationship with Bell Bank Park allows us to be in the center of the action without incurring liability. We have overcome challenges and are on our way to creating a unique curriculum. Although we'll face competition and imitation in the future, we'll take that as a compliment. Overall, we look forward to moving forward and continuing to develop our innovative approach to education.

Our program is geared toward three types of students. First, we have students from the community who come to us because of the school's proximity. Second, we offer an international component, primarily online, with residential camps and other activities throughout the year. Finally, we recently entered into an agreement with the International Student Exchange Organization, which will send many international students on exchange to our school.

We can provide experiences for high school and college students through our partnership with Park University. In addition, because Leigh's name is associated with the program, we can attract high-caliber talent, including faculty and potential guest speakers from the world of sports. The collaboration is developing very well and is mutually beneficial.

Finally, our program targets students focused on academic and athletic excellence who desire a boarding school experience. Our approach aims to provide diverse opportunities for students with different backgrounds and interests to ensure a well-rounded educational experience.

We want to help our students succeed in life no matter what path they take. A small percentage may become sports stars, but most won't. By partnering with various organizations, we can support athletes who have had short professional careers and need assistance transitioning into other fields. This population has enormous potential, and we believe we can change their lives.

We also understand the importance of working with stakeholders such as parents, grandparents, and seniors. This growing demographic has valuable experience, free time, and disposable income. They may want to pursue entrepreneurship but lack the knowledge needed to write business plans or secure financing. We plan to offer programs tailored to their needs as well.

Although our primary focus is high school education, we see numerous opportunities to leverage our partnerships and develop complementary skills. By pooling the expertise of all stakeholders, we aim to create a viable and academically rigorous program that addresses the challenges of growing businesses and diverse populations.

About the Author

Envisage Global, led by Dr. Ray Powers, offers continuing education and workforce development options through partnerships with universities and training partners. Their programs are evaluated for college credit equivalency and provide certificates, certifications, and badges. Dr. Powers has over thirty years of corporate experience and holds multiple degrees, including a Doctorate in Educational Leadership.

FOR EVERY BUSINESS & BUDGET

Looking for a website design firm or D.I.Y. platform that can help you build a visually stunning and effective online brand? Look no further than our expert team. At Proshark, we help you build a customized website that meets your unique needs and goals and converts visitors to customers.

PROSHARK SITES

INNOVATION DESIGNED TO INSPIRE

www.proshark.com

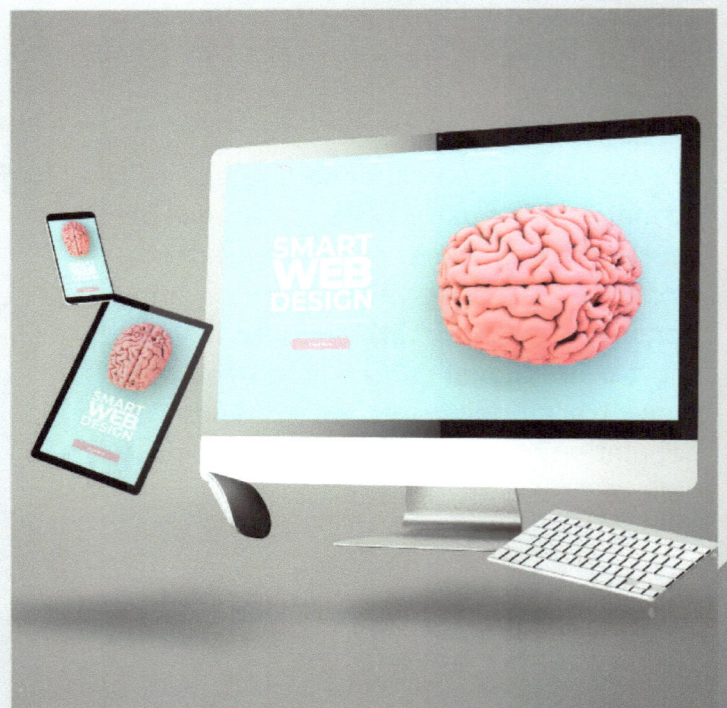

JOHN STRAHL

Leigh Steinberg asked me to join Steinberg Sports because he had spent the previous two years working on and testing modalities of advanced medicine that could mitigate sports injuries. This has been a twenty-year passion of his, starting with concussions. He stayed committed to testing all of these advanced modalities personally so when he spoke about them, it would not only be from the viewpoint of medical studies and clinical evaluations but also from personal experience.

When the initiative was ready to be presented to Steinberg's board, I was asked to come in and head it. One of the members of the team, who had been with them for the last ten years and happened to be an old friend of mine, had invited me. The task entailed building a portfolio of these modalities that would make sense to professional and collegiate sports teams.

Since I arrived, I've been working on this and other everyday activities a president has to deal with. The most advanced modality is the NESTRE and Brain Health Hawaii sciences, which can measure activity in your brain and trace the signaling that occurs in the networks inside your brain.

Once they've identified those networks, they apply a treatment that exposes you to a computer that moves different images around. Your mind automatically starts to seek the formation it knows it should be.

For instance, it's like looking at a moving Rubik's Cube that comes apart, and your brain is already putting it back together. This process is measured in a way that exercises components of your brain, reconnecting tired network cells. The results are simply incredible.

Leigh once lost his memory of names. During testing, they found a dark spot in his brain that shouldn't have been there. After ten or fifteen treatments, the area was clear, and he could remember everybody's name again.

The application of this therapy not only helps you recover from injuries, but it also actually speeds up your reaction time in the brain. Consider how fast Patrick Mahomes is and how quickly he responds to conditions on the field. Then think how untouchable he would be if he sped that up and improved it by 20% or even just 3%. So it's not just healing, but overall improvement as well. Additionally, hyperbaric chambers, red light therapy, and vibration therapy are increasingly being used in sports.

We believe that teams are starting to see that this can't be just a tiny effort or something that happens over in the corner for a while. Instead, it has to be an orchestrated effort so that the whole team is working under the best conditions. The games have reached a point in most professional sports where they're often decided in the last quarter or even on the last play.

This makes a massive difference if you have a one, two, or three-percent edge, especially if your top-string players are on the field, not the bench. The gap between the A and B players is no longer a small gap, primarily because of cap rules and other factors.

One of these technologies uses rTMS as one of the advanced brain modalities in addition to the technology mentioned earlier. rTMS is an electromagnetic device that delivers a rapidly pulsed magnetic field to the brain to activate neurons without inducing seizures. It's used for prescribed conditions of OCD and related issues.

There are plans to use these advanced modalities at the Steinberg Sports Academy. In fact, we believe it's very important that high schoolers begin using these modalities as soon as they start playing sports. Our programs are built around a curriculum that not only teaches these concepts but also incorporates coaching, training, and athletic endeavors that consider all of that.

The Steinberg Sports Academy was conceived before my time. Dr. Ray Powers, the former dean of several universities and also a vice president at AT&T for many years, began dealing with technology and learning. After retiring from AT&T, he started a company that developed enhanced curricula for universities. As time went on, he saw that these curricula could also have an impact on adolescents.

With the turmoil in the education industry, it made sense to focus on areas that would appeal to parents who are, to put it mildly, up in arms about the current education system. They want a voice and something different from what has not been working in the existing system. Taking that into consideration, Dr. Powers developed a higher-order thinking curriculum that infiltrates every subject and creates several electives. In addition, because of our partnership with Park University, students can earn *two years of college credit* upon graduating from high school.

This is a major attraction, especially for students who know they're going to college and are eager to enter sports. The combination of college accreditation and a deeper knowledge of their athletic abilities is valuable. In the process, students learn about their athletic skills and gain insights into how the sports business works. This offers a broad range of potential interests from a professional standpoint. Whether a student wants to be a sports journalist, coach, trainer, or run a sports company, all these possibilities will be part of the sports curriculum.

Because the Steinberg Sports Academy is a new business with partnerships involving highly qualified people, it needs to acquire capital for securing land, building the school, and operating it until it becomes profitable. As the CFO, that's one of my major roles. In addition, my background includes securing funds for startups and taking companies from the $100 million class up to $300 or $400 million in a short period by creating growth cycles.

The Steinberg Sports Academy will be a for-profit organization with the possibility of a future nonprofit division. If charitable

donors who appreciate the programs want to contribute on a charity basis, we would need to file and set up a structure for that. The model looks so promising that we've already had requests from different parts of the country and overseas expressing interest in having a school in their city. As a result, we also have inquiries from prospective students from foreign countries, and we anticipate a reasonably large percentage of our student population will be international. For some people, enrollment in a school overseas is part of their strategy for their child's success.

The ideal student for the Steinberg Sports Academy is one with a high grade-point average who doesn't want to attend a school that doesn't meet the demands for intellectual growth and additional studies. Parental influence is known to support high academic achievements and potential sports involvement that could lead to a professional career in sports. In other words, children who have been playing sports like Pop Warner football, by the time they enter high school, aspire to be on the varsity team as soon as possible. Some of them are already declaring which college they want to attend based on sports and the professional teams they're considering playing for in the NFL, NBA, or MLB. It's a synergy of two high-level, directed interests to create enhanced life opportunities for students.

Of course, as I mentioned earlier, if the educational component of our program overcomes the resistance of parents who are dissatisfied with existing conditions, all the better. We have a grand vision for the future of the Steinberg Sports Academy, which includes replicating it worldwide. One of our partners, Park University, has sixty locations in this country, showcasing an intriguing model.

Though it took Park University a hundred years to achieve this, it still demonstrates what can be accomplished, and in today's world, everything moves more quickly. The fact that we currently have interest from Memphis, Texas, India, and China speaks to the potential of our program.

My advice to parents who appreciate the idea of providing this environment for their child is to talk to someone, learn what's going on, and listen closely.

About the Author

John Strahl, with a bachelor's degree from UCLA and an MBA from UCI, brings extensive experience and expertise in finance and academics to his role as the CFO and the Executive Dean of Academics of Steinberg Sports Academy. Additionally, as President of Leigh Steinberg Sports & Entertainment, he has demonstrated his entrepreneurial skills and expertise in the sports industry.

DR. JULIE DUCHARME

It's been about ten years since I started the Synergy Learning Institute. I was a chair of three different divisions for a university in San Diego. As you may know, San Diego is a military town with both active and retired personnel. Some professors approached me, expressing concern about veterans struggling with various aspects of transitioning back into civilian life.

Initially, I thought they were referring to the challenges of returning to school after a long absence, but the professors clarified that there were other struggles these students faced. I was naive to the issue, as my own family members in the military never seemed to have any difficulties adjusting to

civilian life. However, I may not have been aware of their struggles as a child.

Caught off guard by this revelation, I approached the higher-ups at the school and asked if there was anything we could do to support our veteran students, such as creating a course. However, they were uninterested, claiming no money was in it. I was shocked because I believed that assisting students to succeed in all aspects of their lives would ultimately benefit the school's retention, graduation rates, and job placement outcomes—all factors that could bring in funding. To me, it made sense to find a way to bridge the gap.

Now, many groups are addressing this issue. For instance, Wounded Warriors does an excellent job helping those transitioning back from physical injuries. A long list of organizations is working to support veterans in various ways.

I began immersing myself in the veteran community in San Diego, where I discovered a coalition of around 150 companies offering various forms of support. They provide services such as water therapy, physical therapy, and even a new type of mental boot camp. Unfortunately, while numerous excellent groups exist, each can only handle a limited number of people. On average, we have two million veterans transitioning out of the military each year, with another two million joining—meaning a lot of veterans need support.

Drawing from my twenty-three years of academic experience, I began to think about the educational aspect I could bring to these veterans. I wasn't a psychologist and didn't have much experience working with the military, but I knew that education could bridge gaps in various contexts. For example, we often discuss how education leads to success in low-income communities, and that's where my idea stemmed from. I initially tried to build the program with others, but their military duties prevented them from committing.

My father, a long-time college professor, called me about starting the school during this time. The VA had contacted him about six veterans who needed training but only had a budget of $1,000 per person. He asked if we could do something, and I agreed to figure it out, despite our limited knowledge. My father, an experienced automotive instructor, and I, with my extensive academic background, joined forces. The veterans we were assisting had all worked in some capacity in automotive divisions within the military.

We created a course for these veterans with the help of my father and professors from Bakersfield College. We held the classes in a hotel in Bakersfield, using the conference room for lessons and the parking lot for hands-on demonstrations with cars. Our students ranged in age and experience from sixty-year-olds to a twenty-year-old who had worked as a plane mechanic.

After completing the program, we held a small graduation ceremony at the hotel, where I personally handed out certificates. We then assisted the graduates in finding jobs. This first program was a success, and we wanted to develop it further. However, the cost of creating a full-scale automotive program was exorbitant. Establishing such a program required hundreds of thousands of dollars for facilities and equipment.

We attempted to collaborate with other colleges, but we encountered resistance. They were not interested in pursuing this type of program. Consequently, we put our automotive program on hold, as we had only been operating for six months and lacked the necessary funding. I returned to San Diego, where I continued to explore partnerships with various organizations.

I began by exploring partnerships with existing organizations so as not to reinvent the wheel. We started collaborating with other groups, meeting the needs of the VA, and gradually developed our own programs. Creating a college was far more challenging than I initially thought, but it was a labor of love.

Over the past twelve years, we have continued to grow, learn, and expand our offerings. We now have thirty-six accredited courses through partnerships with various universities. However, we are not GI Bill-approved, as there are strict requirements, such as being near a military base and running a program continuously for two years. Unfortunately, the COVID-19 pandemic disrupted our ability to meet these requirements.

Despite setbacks, our organization has grown beyond what I could have imagined. We are currently considering our next steps for expansion. As the organization's president, I do not take a salary, and all our current staff members are volunteers. We are exploring ways to transition into a structure that allows full-time salaries so our team can dedicate their complete attention to the school.

Our veterans have a wealth of knowledge and skills to share, and our biggest challenge is helping them recognize that their training surpasses that of most civilians. This realization struck me during a conversation with the Secretary of the Navy and Navy Seals, who pointed out that millions of dollars have been invested in training our veterans.

These individuals emerge from service with extensive training, and we are responsible for harnessing their skills. We emphasize their expertise in leadership, teamwork, logistics, and working under pressure.

In the civilian workforce, veterans have an advantage over other applicants because their military experience has prepared them for challenges far more significant than what they will encounter in most jobs. However, it is essential to help them harness their skills, as they often have a narrow view of their capabilities, focusing only on their specific military roles.

While obtaining a degree from a college is valuable, traditional institutions may not always effectively help veterans translate their military experience into civilian careers. By recognizing their extensive training in areas like logistics and management of valuable resources, we can help veterans leverage their skills.

Our goal is to make an impact without becoming a large, multi-million-dollar institution. As the president of Synergy Learning Institute, my responsibilities include building strategic partnerships, overseeing marketing and budgeting, and finding ways to maximize our resources to benefit our veteran students.

We hope to establish partnerships with organizations like the Steinberg Sports Academy, enabling us to create hubs for veterans at locations such as colleges. These collaborations would allow us to expand our reach and better support our veteran community while remaining a small, agile organization focused on making a meaningful impact.

I believe that networking is crucial for our organization's success. As part of my efforts, I attend monthly SD Mac meetings and participate in a coalition of over 150 veteran groups. Additionally, I regularly engage with various department heads, both active and non-active, to understand their needs and explore potential partnerships.

We hope to reestablish our presence on military bases, like Camp Pendleton, as COVID restrictions ease. Securing a space on base would allow us to work closely with military personnel nearing their transition to civilian life. With our institute located near four bases, we plan to rebuild and strengthen our connections with these military communities.

Of course, securing grants and funding remains a priority. Our next goal is to allocate resources to hire full-time staff, allowing the organization to grow. Our team volunteers their time, and I am involved in nearly every aspect of the nonprofit. I didn't anticipate such growth when I first began this venture, but it underscores the significant need for our services. Instead of focusing on building a multi-million-dollar facility, we prioritize providing essential services for veterans.

We have expanded our services to focus on women veterans, an underserved demographic in the United States. Currently, only about five or six programs nationwide cater specifically to this group. This highlights a significant need for more targeted support.

One of our key partnerships is with Save the Girls, an organization that addresses critical needs for women veterans and women experiencing domestic violence and homelessness. Last year, they distributed 90,000 bras and 300,000 menstrual products, showcasing the demand for these essential items. We are also working on a program called The Nation, which aims to provide food, diapers, and baby formula for women veterans in crisis.

Our goal is to offer educational resources, direct services, and support through our partners. For instance, if a woman veteran in San Antonio, Texas, requires assistance, we can direct her to a local pantry for supplies. We are also creating clothing pantries for women seeking professional attire for job interviews. The transition from military life can be challenging, and the financial strain can be especially acute in areas like San Diego, where the cost of living is high.

Given the steep housing costs and other expenses such as transportation and gas, we need to provide a comprehensive support system for women veterans in need. Our goal is to help ease their transition and empower them to succeed in their post-military lives.

Statistics indicate that around 80 to 90 percent of women transitioning out of the military are single mothers, presenting unique challenges. We have partnered with organizations that specialize in supporting these women in the past, but many of these groups are now at capacity. Consequently, we recognized the need to expand our efforts and work with our community to create support hubs.

One area in which veterans often need assistance is with job interviews and resume writing. While they possess valuable skills, transitioning to a civilian job market can be difficult. For example, we recently encountered a resume with no white space, crammed with information in in a tiny font.

photo credit Ira Bowman of Bowman Digital Media

Although the candidate had impressive qualifications, potential employers would likely overlook the presentation.

To address this issue, we are focusing on expanding our programs and partnering with community members who can help teach veterans essential job-seeking skills, such as interviewing and resume writing. Our women's program, in particular, stands out as a unique and vital aspect of our over-all mission.

I became involved in the Steinberg Sports Academy through my collaboration with Dr. Ray Powers, who had partnered with us to accredit our courses at Synergy Learning Institute. Ray and I share a passion for education and noticed that the system was beginning to falter. We observed a tendency to push students through without address-ing their needs and a reluctance to explore alternative educational methods.

Dr. Powers envisioned a school that would embrace STEAM (science, technology, engi-neering, arts, and math) and project-based learning, transforming students' learning. Many schools understand these effective methods, but financial constraints often hinder implementation. So when he shared his idea for the Steinberg Sports Academy, I eagerly joined the effort, knowing I could contribute my experience building schools and my dedication to education.

As a parent of two school-aged children, making a positive impact on education is my personal mission. It is not enough to merely complain about the system; taking action is essential. By establishing a private school, we can maintain greater control and avoid the limitations imposed by district-run institutions.

Launching the Steinberg Sports Academy has been challenging, but we are close to securing the necessary funding. Our team is working tirelessly to bring this vision to life, and the expertise of Leigh Steinberg and his associates has proven invaluable in our efforts.

When building an endeavor like this, having influential connections like Leigh Steinberg, who can bring in prominent figures such as Warren Moon and Ray Lewis, is invaluable. In addition, their involvement catches the attention of parents and children, helping to spread the word.

Ray asked me if I had the time for this project, but I knew I had to make time because I passionately believed in it. My skill set complements Ray's, and our strong mutual trust creates an exceptional working environment. As the Chief Academic Officer, I am responsible for forging strategic partnerships with companies like Under Armour and Nike and individuals interested in creating endowment funds for student scholarships. This role aligns perfectly with my abilities, personality, and professional network.

My academic background and experience designing courses and running schools also contribute to the project. In addition, I bring valuable sports knowledge and connections as a former professional athlete and seasoned coach. We can leverage our combined expertise to benefit the academy by

working alongside Leigh Steinberg. By connecting with the community and organizing sports camps, we can provide exceptional coaching opportunities, even for those who cannot attend our school.

Within my role as chief academic officer, there are numerous other aspects to oversee. Currently, I'm focusing on three major areas. As we grow, we'll likely hire individuals for specific roles, but for now, as with any startup, everyone pitches in and does what needs to be done.

The design of the Steinberg Sports Academy is similar to IMG Academy in Florida, which is an outstanding institution. However, we've expanded our vision to include sports and a strong emphasis on academics, particularly in STEAM fields. While our programs are not yet operational, our goal is to provide students with opportunities to learn about business, entrepreneurship, audio and video production, photography, and more.

We want our students to graduate with a four-year degree, a two-year college degree, and the additional skills our unique programs offer. Our school aims to remove limitations and help students build their dreams. Instead of the traditional path of attending college and working in a single job for thirty years, we encourage students to find their passions, learn about them, and pursue them upon graduation. If they want to start their own businesses at eighteen, they'll have the skills to do so.

Our ultimate vision is to have investors ready to support students with promising ideas as they graduate. We want to showcase our students' potential to companies like Google, inviting them to hear these young innovators' pitches. This approach is quite different from the traditional academic system, and I've always been passionate about it, especially when it comes to my own children.

My daughter is writing her first book, and both of my children are exploring potential businesses at ages eleven and fourteen. I always remind them that the sky's the limit, and they don't need to wait for permission to be successful. We hope to instill this philosophy in our school, attracting people who share this vision and are committed to nurturing innovation and creativity.

Today, we see young individuals making millions on YouTube, inventing groundbreaking technologies, or even making strides in cancer research. So why not foster that potential in an educational environment. Sports were a significant part of my life and contributed to my success, and while they were the right fit for me, I understand that others may thrive more in academic pursuits.

The Steinberg Sports Academy aims to open doors for students who want to explore their passions, regardless of whether they lie in sports or academics. We believe that students who are serious about chasing their dreams and willing to put in the work will find our school the perfect environment for them.

My vision for the future of the Steinberg Sports Academy involves creating a school that brings together exceptional students and helps them grow. I foresee the school reaching a point where there is a waiting list, with people eager to enroll because of the success and achievements of our students. Ultimately, I envision the school expanding and replicating this model in different parts of the country and even worldwide.

Other nations have already expressed interest in our model, suggesting a universal need for this type of education. People worldwide are searching for ways to help students harness their potential in academics, sports, and personal goals. Our school may become a model that others attempt to recreate, which I have no issue with. Imitation is the sincerest form of flattery, and we can only serve so many students.

By encouraging other institutions to adopt our methods, we can begin a revolution in education. I hope we become a school that attracts teachers, educators, and coaches who want to learn about our approach and implement it in their own school systems. I see a bright future for the Steinberg Sports Academy, although much work must be done.

We have a fantastic network of individuals who are eager to be involved, and I am excited to hire excellent teachers and bring in remarkable coaches. The growing interest in our school indicates we are addressing a genuine need and are on the right path. I am very optimistic about the Steinberg Sports Academy's future and its impact on education.

STRATEGIC GROWTH PROFESSIONALS

We Help Your Business Grow

CONSULTING AGENCY

SERVICE

Online courses

Our courses are strategically designed to assist your business in being recognized by customers, thereby growing your business and achieving long-term revenue streams, as well as how to maintain your competitive edge

Certifications and Contracts

SGP helps you in successfully navigating the complicated path of government contracting by assisting you in obtaining any government certifications you may qualify for and throughout the proposal lifecycle.

Holistic Grant Proposals

Our comprehensive grant proposal services focus on the entire lifecycle, including the development of a repository system.

ABOUT US

At Strategic Growth Professional you are not considered clients, you are considered partners. When we begin working together, it is our partnership that makes each of us successful.

WHY CHOOSE US ?

We are a team of experts and have helped hundreds of people grow their businesses. We have assisted our partners in obtaining over $2 billion in federal, state, and local government contract awards, $1 billion in federal, state, local, foundation, and corporate grant awards, and another $1 billion in private sector awards.

Partnering with you in success

Emily J. McIntyre
Strategic Growth Professionals
O: 719.504.4190
C: 719.257.1981
info@strategicgrowthprofessionals.com
www.strategicgrowthprofessionals.com

COACH ANTHONY STONE

From a young age, I dreamt of becoming a professional athlete—just like most kids, right? However, during high school, I decided that if I couldn't make it as a professional football player or into the pros, I wanted to impact children's lives by teaching them. I wanted to share what I had learned from my own experiences and my teachers because, to me, teaching is priceless. That's why I chose the field of education. Those priceless moments with kids, like watching them serve a volleyball over the net for the first time, make it all worthwhile. All the other kids cheer for their peer, and moments like that inspired me to become a teacher.

How long have I been teaching? Well, I like to see it the opposite way. I have about thirteen and a half more years left. People often ask why I look at it that way, and it's because I enjoy a good countdown. A countdown is like a celebration to me.

I have a lot of stories from the twenty years I've been teaching. I've had the pleasure of watching kids play sports and grow as individuals. I initially taught elementary school and then moved on to middle school. I've been at my current school since 2009, and I've witnessed the growth of my students in various settings, like the weight rooms in town where I work out.

Seeing their progress is fantastic, but it's the personal stories that truly stand out. Some students have told me that if it weren't for my encouragement, they wouldn't have tried out for high school or middle school volleyball or basketball. One student I taught during science class now runs a successful business selling dogs. We used to discuss his dogs in class, and today, he sells them at astounding prices. Unfortunately, when he told me the price of a dog, I had to decline—I couldn't spend as much on a dog as I did on my car!

I currently teach four children whose parents I taught in middle school. As a result, there are countless stories from my teaching career, and it's impossible to pick just one. If I were to share a specific story, others might ask, "Why didn't you tell mine?" But the stories I've mentioned provide a general idea of my experiences.

As for coaching, I've been at it for about twenty-five years. I recently celebrated a birthday, and I owe my start in coaching to Dennis Worsall, one of my high school coaches. He introduced me to the sport as a sophomore, teaching me to play and coach. As a quarterback, you must be a leader both on and off the field, which sometimes involves coaching your fellow players. So whenever someone asks me that question, I reflect on my beginnings.

I say I've been coaching for twenty-five years, but it's actually been a little longer than that. I was a sophomore about thirty years ago, but I count twenty-five years because, during college, I worked at camps where I coached kids. Along the way,

memorable stories and events demonstrate the value of sports experiences for kids.

One story that comes to mind is from my second year of coaching high school football. I was working at a local high school and recruiting players. I met a young man who I encouraged to play football, and he became a Division III athlete, an All-American, and an All-Academic. After moving to Tennessee, he became a physical education teacher and a coach. He even bought several of my books and worked for my company.

Later, he became a defensive coordinator at a Division III college and eventually took a job as the head football coach at his alma mater, where I had initially recruited him. This is one of the most successful stories I've been a part of. I remember telling him he couldn't play quarterback due to his size. But he was a tall baseball player who was a great athlete. Now, he trains my son and has co-authored a strength and conditioning book with me.

I also think camaraderie is crucial for kids. Growing up, I had an older brother and was fortunate to play sports with him. Despite our six-year age difference, I could keep up with him as I grew taller. The camaraderie, new friendships, and brotherhood or sisterhood formed through sports are invaluable. I've coached women's football too, and it's all about that family-like connection.

I often say it's like an extension of your family. Those bonds never fade, whether it's reaching out to ask questions or offering support. This sense of unity—this brother or sisterhood—persists. Years later, people still reach out to me when I coach or host a camp.

My company, Coach Stone Football, was established in the winter of 2017. My wife and I were discussing the idea, and she came up with the name. I noticed many parents were being thrust into volunteer coaching positions as youth coaches, so my business started creating customized camps. Essentially, I parachute in, conduct a camp, and then parachute out, hoping to lay a solid foundation where one might not have existed before.

In any business, it's crucial to have a strong foundation. You can't build on sand; it needs to be concrete. Otherwise, the structure will just keep sinking. So my wife suggested that I pursue this venture, and so I did, focusing on building a foundation and boosting confidence through drills. This starkly contrasts the old days when kids who got answers wrong were made to run a mile, only to be brought back and forced to do it again if they messed up.

Nowadays, we approach coaching differently, recognizing that kids are not merely conditioned athletes but individuals with unique talents. My company aims to lay a foundation for growth, build confidence, and use sports or other activities to achieve that. For example, I began traveling with a company and creating football camps for them. Word spread, and I eventually went out alone, finding great success.

Before COVID hit, I would conduct about ten camps a year. Now that the situation is improving, I've completed four camps and scheduled more. So the future looks promising for Coach Stone Football as we continue to empower young athletes through sports and confidence-building activities.

I had to cancel two camps because I had a dance recital for three of my five children. I couldn't do the camp, as I wanted to see my kids participate in their activities. With my oldest daughter, I missed seeing her grow up while focusing on my career, and I don't want to make that mistake again.

Since then, I've made it a point to attend all my children's events, whether my oldest daughter's track and field, flag football, or my son's football game. In addition, I'm always there for my third child's basketball games, either on the bench or cheering from the stands. I also missed a camp when I attended my fourth daughter, Chloe's, school play.

I'm grateful to those who contact me for camps, but I have to prioritize my family. Sometimes, I decline bookings due to dance recitals, plays, or other family commitments. My youngest daughter is now exploring acting and is always eager to share her school stories with me. The time I spend with my children is priceless and worth the effort to balance my professional and personal life.

I also work for Jen Welter's company, although she's currently on hiatus with the XFL, coaching the Vegas Vipers alongside Coach Woodson. I was fortunate enough to attend their first home game, for which I'm genuinely grateful. Interestingly, my daughter had a basketball game that day, but she gave me permission to see Jen's game instead since I had missed one of her games previously.

Jen's Gridiron Girl camps, which I've had the pleasure of participating in, are fantastic. The Camp on the Corner initiative she created and everything else she does is incredible. She has become like a family member in our household. We have shared many memorable experiences with her, such as taking her to a Chicago Bears event.

Jen's accomplishments in women's sports are astounding and deserve recognition, like her ESPN special. She broke significant barriers as the first female professional football player, then went on to launch Gridiron Girls camps. Five or six years ago, there were no flag camps for girls, but now they can be found everywhere. I had the privilege of joining her in Australia, where she was the head coach, and I served as the defensive coordinator and assistant football coach.

I was fortunate to collaborate with her on camps hosted by the New York Giants, New York Jets, and the Rams. Although I've had to miss some camps, I've had many amazing experiences with Jen, such as the mom's clinic for the NFL with the Washington Redskins and Santana Moss, which we conducted a while back.

I've spoken with others about her, and I can confidently say that her football IQ is through the roof. She truly knows her stuff and is an excellent teacher when it comes to tackling. I loved watching her demonstrate tackling techniques with Harry Connick Jr. on his show.

I have nothing but great things to say about her. If she ever decides to return to the NFL, I hope she gets the opportunity. Currently, she's serving as the linebackers coach for the Vegas Vipers, but I know she enjoys being on the field.

Our connection began when I met her after an All-Star game where I had been the head coach. We've known each other since 2010, and she has steadily made strides in her career. I remember when she told me she was joining the Arizona Cardinals. I was at a football camp when she told me to turn on ESPN—and there she was. It was a fantastic moment.

I've also written a lot of books. Surprisingly, it took me years and years to write my "Big Four" book, which is relatively small, while my green book, about 500 pages thick, only took about two months to write. I had everything outlined, and it made the process smoother. If you're ever thinking about writing a book, I advise you to write down your ideas and only write when you feel inspired. Forcing yourself to write may not yield the best results.

Currently, I have three completed books for which I'm just waiting on covers and proofreading. Because I'm dyslexic, writing takes me longer because I see and write things backward. So when people proofread my work, they often ask me what I'm trying to say. Of course, I can say it correctly, but it may not appear that way on paper.

I enjoy writing, and I'm excited about my upcoming books. I'm currently working on two more books. One will be finished after the other three are done; the other is a co-authored book. I've made all my football books affordable for coaches because there wasn't a suitable platform for them at an accessible price point.

There wasn't a platform for these resources before, but now everyone's creating content.

photo credit Ira Bowman of Bowman Digital Media

Since COVID, people have been developing drills and manuals. Even to this day, my first flag book remains the biggest flag book ever made. My green book for drills is part of the most extensive series ever created for tackle football. I have completed volumes one through five of my green book, with the coaching edition as number five, and my sixth book, *Coaching Secrets*, is already done.

Coaching Secrets will reveal all my coaching techniques, even though I've already shared many of them. I want to put everything on paper to help others succeed in football and build kids' confidence because I know I won't remember everything as I get older. To date, I've published one paperback and twenty-four "Back to the Basics" books, including quote books and a DIY book.

It's incredible to see how many DIY books are available now. Since I wrote a DIY book on drills, others have followed suit, and people are also launching academies and other programs. I also started a free magazine for coaches during COVID to give back to the coaching community. Published five times a year, it's an international magazine that showcases coaching tips from around the world, making it a valuable resource for coaches' toolboxes. So far, I've written twenty-five coaching books under the "Back to the Basics" logo.

I worked with a publishing company for my first book before deciding to self-publish the rest. Although it was challenging, I appreciated the company for getting me started. If I had the chance, I would publish all my books through a traditional publisher, especially since some have won awards like "Best eBook of the Year" and "Best Book of the Year."

A couple of months ago, I led a football camp in Mesa, Arizona, at the site of Leigh Steinberg's upcoming Steinberg Sports Academy. I'll support the Steinberg Sports Academy by organizing sports camps to enrich the lives of kids in the Arizona community. When Dr. Julie Ducharme brought me on board, she saw the potential in the customized camps I had run elsewhere. I'm excited about the Academy's plans for the community, the state, and potential student-athletes. It will be a phenomenal experience, and they have a lot of support.

To learn more about me, visit my website at coachstonefootball.com. You can find my shop on my website, see some of my sponsors who help with my camps, and scroll down to view videos and testimonials. You can also follow me on Twitter, Facebook, and Instagram.

In addition, I have a college class coming out soon. If you're interested in camps or books, all my books are available on Amazon. Search for "Back to the Basic Football Drill Manuals," and you'll see my work listed there.

UNLOCK YOUR SUPER BOWL POTENTIAL

CHUKKY OKOBI

As a young kid, I didn't have a vision of playing football. I didn't start playing football until high school when I attended the Trinity-Pawling prep school, about an hour north of New York City. TP is an all-boys school: in any given year, there were only about 260 students when I attended.

Because the school was so small, there were no physical education classes. Instead, to meet the New York State Phys. Ed requirement each student had to play a recreational or competitive sport each season fall, winter, and spring. As a freshman at age thirteen, I had never played fall sports before. Me being a Pittsburgh native, I had a deep love for the Steelers, so football was a natural choice for me in the Fall of 1992.

My passion for sports began at a young age when I was still living in Pittsburgh. Growing up in a difficult home where my parents didn't get along, sports became my escape.

At home, as a child, I often felt unimportant. But when I was on the team, out with my brothers, or playing sports with my friends in the neighborhood, I experienced a deep sense of self-worth. In those moments, I loved myself when I played sports.

Through sports, I discovered this sense of self-worth and love for myself when I was seven, and I really enjoyed being myself when I was playing sports. The positive emotion I felt when playing sports is what led me to definitively decide early in life that I was going to be a professional athlete when I grew up.

My first love as a child was baseball. That was the only organized sport I played up until high school, and that's what I planned on playing when I grew up. My natural athletic abilities were more suited to football, so after two fall seasons at TP, I really began to focus on football.

By junior year, I wouldn't say I was that good at football just yet. As a matter of fact, throughout my sports career, I was never the best player on my team in any sport or at any level. I wasn't the kid you looked at and said, "Oh, he's definitely going to be a star!" But I wanted to be.

The desire to be a pro athlete motivated me and drove me to focus on constant improvement. And still, after my third season, I wasn't being recruited by any colleges. Coming from such a small high school program, I hadn't hit the college recruiting radar. So, after my junior season, I decided to take matters into my own hands and took it upon myself to write a letter to literally every Division I-A school in America

to let them know I was out there and eager to play. I took the initiative and approached the schools myself.

After reaching out to over 110 schools, the lone scholarship offer I received was from Purdue University. I was very grateful because all I was looking for one opportunity.

When I got to Purdue, my new objective was to find out how good I could be. Now that I had an opportunity to play college football at a Big Ten school, I wanted to see if I had a limit, and I found that there are no limits except the ones we set in our minds. I was very focused on becoming a professional athlete, a decision I had made when I was seven. That was always the plan.

In college, I didn't get so involved in social activities. I focused on making sure I was prepared for my duties as an athlete. That included academic responsibilities because that's what you have to do when you play college football. Maintaining my eligibility to play was always a priority.

I focused on taking care of myself physically and mentally and preparing myself to do well in practice and games. With that mindset, especially after everything I had gone through to get the opportunity to play college football, I was very focused.

In my freshman year, I redshirted and didn't play in 1996. Then, in 1997, we changed coaching staff, and I was the only freshman starter on our team. All the effort and focus I put in to impress the new coaching staff allowed me to become a starter at age eighteen. I played the offensive line all four years I played in college. I was also a starter all four years at Purdue. I was an all-Big Ten player as a sophomore, and as a senior, I helped Purdue win only the second Big Ten football championship and Rose Bowl berth in school history. Then, after my senior year, I participated in the Hula Bowl, the NCAA's official all-star game at that time, al of which led to me being drafted into the NFL.

My college years were when my life started to become what I had envisioned it to be at seven. – what I had dreamed and imagined for so long began to come to life. But, as the saying goes, Rome wasn't built in a day.

To become a good player, you need mental and emotional discipline above all. In my work in my speaking and coaching company, *Basic Instructions Mind Mastery*, I coach and train business leaders and companies to develop and master their minds to master their life and career.

I was never the best player on my team at any level. Just think about some of the guys we played with in college, like Super Bowl champion Drew Brees, three-time Super Bowl champion Matt Light, and two-time Super Bowl champion Brandon Gorin. I was the shortest, but I was definitely the strongest. Instead, I saw myself as the heartbeat, the emotional leader who motivated the group and set the tempo and brought everyone together.

I think that taking on that leadership role at Purdue really made a difference. I imagine that trait of emotional leadership contributed to the Steelers wanting me on their team and in their organization and how inquisitive NFL scouting departments were.

For me, it's all about understanding the internal functions of our mind and how we think to get results. I believe we need to think on a higher level than just the physical aspects of sports. We focus so much on the physical body, but the mind controls the physical body. It's really about focusing on mindset, learning how to ignite your emotions and direct them toward a positive goal. That way, you can transfer that energy to the rest of the team so they can do the same.

That approach contributed to our Big Ten championship, and I think it was a good strategy. When I've coached college football players looking for opportunities to play at the next level, I've told them they have to become NFL players in their minds if they want to be selected. This idea may seem confusing at first, but keep in mind that there are about 240 players selected on draft day.

There are at least 10,000 college football graduates in any given year, and not everyone in the draft is a graduate. To get noticed, you have to provide enough value to your team that you stand out. For example, if another team is scouting Purdue football, they should mention your name. If you're an offensive player, opposing defenses should be told about you. They should talk about the difference you make for your team.

To do that, you have to evolve and decide that's who you are now, not who you will be. You can't wait until you get drafted; you have to display an NFL player's behaviors, attitudes, and beliefs right now. I've never seen anyone who didn't believe they could get to the next level. It starts with becoming an NFL player on the inside. How the world sees you on the outside depends on who you're on the inside. That's what you have to do to make it to the next level.

I don't know precisely how scouting works in professional sports. All I know is that during my college career, regional scouts from various NFL teams often came to our practices. Over time, you get to know some of them because they were always there.

Of course, it helped to have Drew Brees as a quarterback to draw attention. He made sure there were a lot of eyes on the TV screens on Saturday afternoon. Playing with Drew got us more attention because everyone was looking at him because he was incredibly skilled and entertaining.

But we were there, too. A quarterback doesn't have time to throw without us. So everyone saw our value and how we enabled Drew to be as good as he was. After that, I made sure the scouting departments took notice because I was playing at a level they couldn't overlook, and everything else seemed to fall into place.

For me, my NFL experience was an extension of my experience as a seven-year-old. It all feels like one journey.

The lesson here is that despite the difficulties at home, I had to let go of the past to focus on where I wanted to go. Those difficulties at home led me to make that decision very early in life, and I never lost sight of that goal.

When I had the opportunity in college and eventually transferred to the Steelers, my hometown team, I kept working to see how good I could be. Some people play in the NFL for eight years, while others don't make it eight days. So every day, I had to keep pushing myself to see how good I could be because new players came in every year.

I started thinking about how much more valuable and fiery I could be with the Steelers, just like I had been at Purdue. That attitude eventually helped our team win a championship in college, and I was part of a team that won a world championship and secured the Super Bowl with the Steelers. The key is to connect with what's happening inside of you and understand your vision for yourself and your life beyond the game.

It's important to remember that we play the sport; the sport doesn't play with us. Sport isn't who you are; it's something you do.

You must focus on improving what's happening inside you to succeed in business or sports. This is because the mind commands and the body obeys. The most important thing I took away from my time in the NFL was the emotions I experienced after achieving my biggest goal in life so far.

People often say to me, "Wow, you were born in Pittsburgh, played for the Steelers, and won the Super Bowl. That's got to be an incredible feeling, right?" Yet, it's a feeling we all know deep down. We all have memories of exciting moments when our pulse is racing, our breath is shallow, and our heart is pounding in our ears.

So if you can recall a memory like that, you know exactly what it feels like to win the Super Bowl. The fascinating thing about

photo credit Ira Bowman of Bowman Digital Media

that moment, witnessing the celebration, the cameras clicking and flashing, the confetti falling, and the tears of joy on the faces of the Steelers' faithful, was the feeling of electricity that went through my body. It was like I never knew I could feel this good. But suddenly, at that moment, I stopped and thought, "Is this it? Is this the peak of the positive emotional vibration I'm going to feel?" At twenty-seven years old, I couldn't help but wonder if the rest of my life would be all downhill.

You asked me about the connection between my leadership and my experiences. The basis of my approach is to pass on the exhilarating feeling I had on that memorable day to every person I meet. I strive to relive that feeling every day. Why can't we experience this feeling over and over again?

Why can't we as people experience that Super Bowl feeling in our jobs, in our businesses, in our personal lives, relationships, and families? That's what the basic instructions I offer are all about.

That's exactly what I train companies and leaders to do, and it's the same approach that led me to my greatest success as an athlete. I may have won the Super Bowl, but the sensation I achieved is what I call the Super Bowl-level result. It goes beyond football. Football is a human experience. The joy, pageantry, backdrop, and energy of the NFL are something we can use in our lives and businesses.

Having achieved my ultimate goal, my mission in life is to show others how to do the same and that it's not complicated. It's all about basic instructions. If you follow them, this simple feeling can become the new paradigm and vibration of your life and business.

Not long ago, I participated in the Steinberg football camp. As a kid, I never had the chance to do something like that. The camp focused on the basics and foundations. To have the success I experienced as an athlete, you have to master those fundamentals.

To truly excel, you have to work tirelessly to master the fundamentals, possibly for the next decade or more. For some kids, that's the journey they're just starting.

It was refreshing to shift the focus from the spectacular skills of football players and show the kids that they, too, can be successful. If they can master the fundamentals of the sport, stay focused, and envision who they want to become, they can achieve the same success as former NFL players. We're no different than them, and there is nothing we can't attain.

What impressed me the most was the confidence the kids gained after the football camp. Their newfound belief in their potential is more important than their athletic ability. That's what got me into the draft. When I reflect on my journey, my unwavering belief in my abilities propelled me forward.

My goal was to teach kids that they can be, do, and have anything they want if they stick to the basics, learn the fundamentals, and stay committed. Steinberg Sports Academy will soon open its doors. As a former private school student, I can attest to the benefits of attending a smaller, specialized facility with a more comprehensive curriculum than a traditional high school.

The Steinberg name is synonymous with excellence in sports. Students attending this academy not only receive a top-notch education but also experience a professional sports culture. The curriculum goes beyond ABCs and 123s and fosters an understanding of the mentality and culture of professional sports so that students can develop that mentality at a young age.

Not all of them will become professional athletes, but they can acquire the mentality, discipline, and focus necessary for excellence in sports. By learning the mental and emotional disciplines at Steinberg Sports Academy, these students will develop the ability to achieve world-class results that will carry over into every aspect of their lives.

This facility has the potential to make a real difference for many children who want to discover their true potential. The overall goal of my work aligns with this mission: to help people reach their full potential.

As a society and as individuals, we are often concerned with the physical aspects of sports or life in general. Sometimes it's not about sports at all but about the superficial aspects of life, such as being associated with big names or companies. In reality, it's all about how you see yourself and what you believe in.

Take, for example, a startup with an idea in the tech industry. You'll never make it if you don't believe in your abilities or that your idea is good enough to compete with Google and Apple. This lack of belief is your own fault, not the fault of external factors.

The same principle applies whether you want to be a doctor, president, or CEO. Have you ever seen someone achieve great success in business without believing they could do it? We need to get back to the basics of who we're as people and understand that we control our own outcomes. Whether you want to win the Super Bowl or make a million dollars, the process is much less complex than it seems.

Just like Dorothy's trip home to Kansas, achieving high success in business or sports may seem complex, but it's simple if you understand the basic instructions. Success is simple, but people are complex. My mission is to simplify success and enable people to follow the basic instructions to reach

Super Bowl levels in their relationships, health, fitness, spirituality, or career. The feeling remains the same.

To learn more about me and my services as a business leadership coach and motivational speaker, visit chukkyokobi.com or basicinstructions.com. The same fire and passion I brought to my team in Pittsburgh, I want to bring to your business.

About the Author

Chukky is a versatile professional who excels as a keynote and motivational speaker, corporate leadership and sales trainer, and master practitioner of integrative psychology. With a background that includes an eight-year NFL career and a Super Bowl XL Championship in 2005, Chukky brings a unique perspective to his various roles, inspiring individuals and teams to achieve their personal and professional goals.

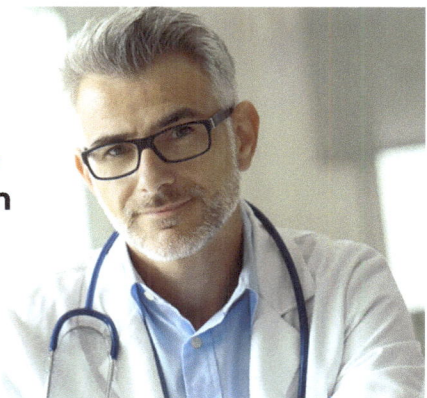

FROM FLAG FOOTBALL TO THE NFL

REGGIE WALKER

My childhood was enjoyable, though I often perceived it as chaotic. We moved around frequently, ultimately spending most of our time in Bloomville, Missouri, and Sacramento, California. My parents served in the military, and my father's career lasted longer than my mother's. Consequently, there were periods when they were away.

Despite the chaos, my childhood was overall positive. I discovered my passion for football at a young age, around four years old. It was an instant attraction, and I remember asking my father about it. He explained that it was a football game, and I could become one of those players if I wanted to. At the time, the players seemed like mythical creatures to me. Soon after, I began playing flag football when I was in kindergarten.

Throughout high school, I played various sports. Essentially, I participated in athletics until I graduated. However, one sport I particularly loved was rugby. I adored it so much that I seriously considered pursuing it further.

I had an opportunity to try out for the Under-19 team, but my high school coach warned me that if I did, I would be benched for the season's first three games. Consequently, I decided not to try out, which I now regret because the team traveled the world, and it would have been an incredible experience.

Rugby is such an enjoyable sport, and the community aspect is one of its best features. The camaraderie and environment were fantastic, making it one of the most memorable times of my life.

The players were all a little crazy but in the best way possible. After a match, we would drink from a shoe and then gather in our cliques before having a joint party with both teams. It was a fantastic experience, and I genuinely miss rugby.

When choosing a college, I didn't prioritize football opportunities; instead, I selected the school farthest from home that had recruited me. I grew up watching Kansas State, having spent time in Bloomville, Missouri, and Kansas when the team was ranked number one in the country and dominating. So while I became a fan, the primary reason for my choice was the school's distance from home.

Upon being recruited after high school, I committed to Kansas State during my visit. I was part of the first year where students receiving scholarships could enroll early; previously, they had to wait until the fall semester. Consequently, I enrolled in the spring, played spring football, and even flew back to attend my high school graduation.

Enrolling early was a new opportunity, and I was among the first to experience it. Now, many students with scholarships take advantage of enrolling in the spring.

My college career was a rollercoaster. I never started more than half a season at Kansas State University during any of my four years. This was mainly due to the political nature of college sports. When the coach who had recruited me retired, and a new coach arrived, I found myself in a situation similar to Deon Sanders' college experience. The new coach wanted me gone, as he preferred to win with his own recruits.

Many people don't realize that in the college sports environment, coaches want to win with the players they've personally recruited. Winning with someone else's recruits could tarnish their victories in their own minds or in the eyes of others. Thus, during my last three years at Kansas State, the coaching staff tried everything to make me quit.

I would make big plays in games, such as sacks or interceptions, only to be taken out immediately afterward. The coaches couldn't stand seeing me succeed. When it came time to train for the NFL after my senior year, I discovered that I had been labeled with major red flags. My film was impressive, but scouts were puzzled about why I would make a big play and then be taken out on the next play.

They didn't understand that the coaches had been trying to break me every day.

However, overcoming these challenges ultimately helped prepare me for the NFL.

Kansas State provided the best experience of my life; I had the time of my life there. The community was incredibly welcoming, and they genuinely considered me a part of the Wildcat community.

One memorable story occurred during my freshman year. Our coach, Bill Snyder, was preparing to retire for the first time. I had the opportunity to play in his last game, which was at home against Missouri. Throughout the season, it had been challenging for me to get consistent playing time as a true freshman due to Coach Snyder's preference not to play true freshmen. However, he recognized my potential and allowed me to play.

In this final game, the plan was for me to play extensively, and I was thrilled to end the season on a high note. I made several tackles for loss, nearly had an interception, and forced a fumble that became one of the game's pivotal moments. At the end of the game, I shook Coach Snyder's hand and told him that my performance was dedicated to him.

I'll never forget the genuine gratitude in his eyes as he thanked me. I have immense respect and admiration for Bill Snyder, a truly remarkable man.

I majored in history for three years, particularly enjoying learning about the Renaissance. However, I eventually faced the fact that I didn't want to be a professor, lawyer, teacher, researcher, or librarian. Unsure of the value of my degree, I decided to switch to family studies and human services to become a social worker, as I enjoyed helping people.

Yet, I didn't finish that degree either. In each class, the instructors would emphasize that social work is a high-burnout profession with an average career span of only four years. In addition, many professionals in the field often struggle with substance abuse problems. They said we could pursue this career if we really wanted to but recommended caution.

Ultimately, I didn't complete the degree. Instead, I went on to play in a league and continued to ponder my career path.

A couple of years ago, I finished my degree in social science, intending to go to grad school to earn a master's in counseling and become a guidance counselor. However, while pursuing my master's, I dropped out to focus on professional sports. Eventually, I improved to the point where teams took notice and considered giving me a chance. Some teams said I might be drafted late, but I wasn't sure what would happen.

Around the fourth round, the Cardinals called and said they were considering picking me up in the sixth or seventh round. However, the sixth round came and went without my being drafted, as did the seventh. During the seventh round, the Cardinals called again, inviting me to join as a free agent with a chance to make the team during training camp. I also received similar offers from four other teams.

Though I went undrafted, this was a pivotal moment for me. I had the opportunity to choose my situation from five different

photo credit Ira Bowman of Bowman Digital Media

teams, which is a significant benefit of being undrafted. Most players who are drafted, like a running back, might end up on a team with two other players competing for the same position. I chose the most beneficial path for me, and I think that decision played a significant role in helping me get into the league.

When I arrived at training camp, something just clicked. I remember participating in the summer training with all the rookies and feeling intimidated because I was among the best of the best. There was no higher platform, and I was in awe of being there. I saw people of all ages, from young guys like me to seasoned veterans.

Despite my initial intimidation, something inside me shifted. I realized no one expected me to accomplish anything or make an impact. However, I knew I would prove them wrong every day. I consistently performed well at camp, and my efforts continued into the preseason games. It was an incredible experience.

I recall having three goal-line stands and making some impressive plays, like jumping over the line to stop an opponent, reminiscent of a scene from a movie. I tackled a player on the one-yard line, which felt like something out of "Little Giants." I continued making these extraordinary plays throughout camp.

I realized I had made the team during our third game when I knocked an opposing player out. As I walked to the sideline, people assured me I had done more than enough to secure my spot on the team.

They encouraged me to relax and not worry about the dreaded cut day.

When cut day finally arrived, I found myself in the meeting room, looking around at all the empty chairs. Half the team had been let go, and the remaining players made up a group much smaller than a college team, let alone an NFL team. Yet, as I surveyed the room, I couldn't help but think that someone would approach me soon.

We then met with the position coach, who told us we could leave and return on Monday. I spoke with my coach afterward and asked, "So, am I good?" He replied, "Yeah, man, you made the team." I hesitated, "So it's okay for me to show up on Monday?" He laughed and said, "Yeah, you better show up on Monday. Enjoy it; you deserve it. You did it, man."

I remember feeling shocked because I knew I was one of the few people who could have accomplished something like that, especially in such a challenging situation as being an undrafted player. They had just gone to the Super Bowl the year before, so this was an excellent team. I felt incredibly proud of myself for what I had achieved.

I made the decision that I was not going to walk in fear. Yes, I was intimidated, being around legendary players like Kurt Warner and others I had only seen on TV. But I remember thinking, "I'm going to challenge everything. If I'm scared, I'll run straight toward it as fast as possible and give it my all. If I win, I win; if I lose, I lose. I'll pick myself up, but I won't be a coward. I will get what I want, and if that takes going above

and beyond, I'll stretch myself until I reach that point." And that's what I did, on repeat, for seven years.

Each of the seasoned players treated rookies differently. Sure, there was rookie hazing, like carrying the guys' pads or having to buy breakfast from Cracker Barrel every Friday and paying for it. At one team dinner, the bill was around $30,000, and three of us had to split it. But for the most part, aside from the occasional comments about being a young buck or just a baby, they showed respect—especially if you gave it to them.

Recently, I had the opportunity to participate in the first football camp hosted by Leigh Steinberg as part of his upcoming Steinberg Sports Academy. It went exceptionally well. The camp was well-organized, and Coach Stone did an excellent job with scheduling and coordination.

The kids were fantastic. We had ample time to teach them good habits for the future and provide them with the tools needed to succeed. Moreover, it was great to have one-on-one conversations with the kids and engage in group discussions at the end of the camp.

The best part was witnessing the children's enthusiasm for learning and determination to improve. It was refreshing to see their curiosity, and it reminded me of myself at that age. I'm grateful to have had the chance to speak with the young athletes; they genuinely listened and appreciated our guidance, demonstrating their eagerness to learn.

The concept behind the Steinberg Sports Academy is ingenious and much needed. I've had private conversations with Leigh about his thoughts on starting the school and what he aims to achieve with it. When we discussed how we could potentially assist him in accomplishing those goals, it was clear that he understood the unique needs of athletes.

Leigh recognizes that providing athletes with specific resources and guidance at an early stage can significantly impact their success in college or professional environments. It's crucial for them to have this knowledge not only about the sports environment they're about to enter but also in areas such as mental development and entrepreneurship. Athletes can make excellent entrepreneurs, as the qualities needed for entrepreneurial success often align with those found in top athletes.

Leigh has been instrumental in securing major deals for athletes, not just endorsements but also business opportunities. He understands the importance of offering this kind of support to athletes everywhere. The Steinberg Sports Academy presents a phenomenal opportunity for athletes to access the resources and guidance they need to excel on and off the field.

MY TURBULENT ROAD TO THE NFL

CHARMEACHEALLE MOORE

My dad was a football player when I was born in 1993. He was on the tail end of his career but still striving to make it to the NFL, playing semi-pro ball. So from the moment I left the womb, I attended games and practices and went into locker rooms. So you could say I was born into football. I still remember taking in the distinct smell. That's one of the things I still do today. I put on my dad's helmet or my own, and just that smell of the equipment is phenomenal.

I started playing contact football at five years old in South Dallas and have been playing ever since then. One of the things that set me apart from many kids today is that I didn't play sports just for fun. That wasn't a thing in my house. We played sports to win, and whatever we did, we didn't quit. We always gave 110% and looked for ways to win. That's the attitude that was embedded in us.

I carried that throughout my career, and it truly helped me when I entered college and faced various scenarios and life challenges. Of course, I could have avoided these challenges, and some people might have justified it, but I persevered.

Throughout my childhood, from playing youth football to transitioning to middle school and then high school, I was always part of great teams. My dad never put me on an underperforming team; he always wanted me to play with high-caliber players to sharpen my skills. This principle of constant improvement was something he instilled in me from an early age. He taught me never to shy away from competition or someone I thought was better than me. They put their pants on like I do, one leg at a time. When you line up across from your opponent, one of you will fold, and he made sure I knew it better not be me.

I remember starting to play varsity during my junior year of high school and getting recruited. I felt on top of the world. I was playing DM, and I'm an undersized DM, but my team was so good that I had to be able to fit in where I could play. I had a great position coach, Terrell Robinson.

One of the core lessons that Coach Rob, my dad, and other great coaches like Coach Jason Todd and Coach Samples taught me was the importance of adopting a dog mentality, but not that of a dumb dog. A dumb dog simply barks at cars, chases them down, and then runs home after reaching the car. Instead, we must be smarter about overcoming challenges and maintain a focused, laser-like determination to achieve our goals.

I committed to the University of Minnesota with Coach Tim Brewster during my junior year. I was drawn to the University of Minnesota after visiting during the summer when the weather was 80 degrees, and the campus was beautiful. At that time, the university had just transitioned to an outdoor facility from an indoor facility.

As I walked the field and explored the campus, I knew this was where I could attend school. Five other players from my high school were already at the University of Minnesota. They were doing great things and expecting me to start right away. Now, my football people will love this: When choosing your school, base it on the position you play and the likelihood of getting time on the field.

Many people viewed the Big Ten at the time as smash-mouth football. As a linebacker playing in the Big Ten, you had a great chance of making it to the NFL because you primarily faced running plays rather than the passing plays that are more common now. It's difficult these days to differentiate conferences based on their styles of play, but back in 2001, when I was playing, things were different.

Though it's been only four years since I left the game, a lot has changed. But at that time, the Big Ten was known for smash-mouth football. I loved the Big Ten, Coach Brewster, and the University of Minnesota, so I committed to the school. But unfortunately, in my senior year of high school, Coach Brewster was fired.

My high school coaches told me I needed to change my commitment and look at other schools, but my mom and dad sat me down and told me that picking a school was like picking a wife. There will always be schools out there that look better, but when you make that commitment, that's what you commit to and where you stay. You don't quit what you start.

I loved the University of Minnesota, so I decided to stick with my decision. A week before signing day, Jerry Kill got the coaching job, and my linebacker coach called and said, "Hey, I just wanted to introduce myself and our new staff. Jerry Kill's going to be giving you a call. Can't wait to have you!" Jerry Kill gives me a call and says he doesn't want me. He pulled my scholarship and told me I had to find somewhere else to go. This was a week before signing day!

You must understand that schools typically offer the same scholarship to multiple individuals. Whoever commits first gets the scholarship. If you don't commit to a school or accept the scholarship when offered, four or five others are waiting in line for the same opportunity. In my case, I had over twenty scholarship offers as one of Texas's top one hundred players. However, a week before signing day, only three schools remained interested in me.

Kansas State University was one of my first offers and was among those that continued to show interest. So, during my junior year, I went on a visit to Kansas State University. I met Coach Bill Snyder and toured the school, but ultimately thought, *I am not coming here.* I actually fell asleep when we had our team meeting with Coach Snyder, and he kicked me out. I just didn't think that was the school for me, but it's crazy how God worked it out.

Texas Tech and the University of Miami also expressed interest in me. They said they had me on their radar but hadn't offered a scholarship because I was still committed to the University of Minnesota. They informed me they had a scholarship available, but I would need to wait and see what other players did on signing day. If all went well, they would sign me a week after signing day. Thus, it would be a waiting game.

Kansas State, on the other hand, offered me a grayshirt scholarship. This differed from a traditional scholarship, as it placed me on their list for the following year. With a grayshirt scholarship, I would sign and graduate but not attend the school immediately. Instead, I would go down for the summer workouts but not enroll for the first semester. I could attend a community college or stay on campus and pay for it myself, but I couldn't take a full course load.

Faced with accepting a grayshirt scholarship from Kansas State, one of the first schools to show interest, or waiting to see what Texas Tech and Miami would do, I consulted with my family and prayed about the decision.

I had two great recruiting coaches that were down there pushing me on. Coach Smitty, my recruiting coordinator, and Coach Joe, the athletic director in Arlington, said, "Mike, Kansas State is the place for you." So instead of waiting until signing day, I signed with Kansas State, which is one of the best decisions I have ever made.

If I hadn't gone to Kansas State University, I genuinely don't know if I would have made it to the NFL or had the work mentality I do. I think I was running from Coach Bill Snyder because I knew he would hold me accountable. I knew he didn't care about the bells and whistles and everything I could do on the field.

During this time, there were college coaches who were either more of a grandad college coach or a player's coach—from Kliff Kingsbury's standpoint. I was asked, "Would you rather play for Kliff Kingsbury down at Texas Tech University, or would you rather come and play for Coach Bill Snyder at Kansas State University, who is not a player's coach, and it's his way or the highway?"

Growing up in an inner-city school, I never had many white coaches, which was a significant culture shock for me when I went to college. I only had two white coaches before attending college, and how they interacted with us was not the same as how college coaches engaged with us.

In college, the coaches aimed to mold young players into the best they could be but according to their way. My previous coaches had a similar approach, but they also instilled in us, especially my Dad, that we were men at the end of the day and shouldn't let anyone disrespect us.

Growing up in the South, we had few interactions with white people. They're on that side, we're on this side, and that was just how it was. At Kansas State University, I had three black coaches; the rest were white coaches, and everybody was talking to you the same.

In Dallas, my black coaches would talk to us harshly and push us, while our white coaches were more lenient. However, the roles were reversed when I went to college at Kansas State. My white coaches were the ones calling me out and being tough. I was used to that kind of coaching, but this time it was a white man talking to me instead of a black man. I questioned their intentions: were they talking to me this way because I was black or a player?

During my first days at Kansas State, I got into a fight, and the university threatened to send me home for the semester because they felt it wasn't working out. We had agreed that I would be a grayshirt, but I had the chance to earn a scholarship if I demonstrated my talent and capability by the fall. Unfortunately, although I was doing everything right in terms of my performance in the weight room and on the field, my character was lacking.

I found myself arguing with coaches and going back and forth with them. I didn't see it as disrespectful because I believed in speaking my mind. During our drills, when I would go against another person, my coaches would comment on my performance, saying, "Mike, you're going to let him beat you up? I can't believe you're performing this way." My mentality growing up was always, "I'm not trash. He can't beat me. He's not about that life, and he's not even in my league. Who else do you have lined up before me? No one can touch me out here." This is how we were raised, believing you must own the room.

However, when you transition to a major university with all that anger and aggression,

photo credit Ira Bowman of Bowman Digital Media

you must learn to present yourself professionally. You have to separate your behavior on and off the field and know when to turn it on and off. I didn't know how to do that. I struggled with switching between the two.

After being home for a semester, I returned to Kansas State University. That was one of the most challenging semesters I've ever faced. Growing up in Dallas, I saw many players receive scholarship offers, go off to college, but then return home and not return to school. I heard countless stories from guys in the barbershop and my high school peers, saying things like, "I could

have been this. I could have done that. I was this. I was that."

I never wanted to be that guy. All my other friends away at school were playing ball, some even as freshmen, which is what I was supposed to be doing. As a result, my focus was off. I was too concerned with everyone else's journey and not focused enough on my own.

From a mental standpoint, it was tough for me because people who knew I was doing well would ask, "Why are you back home? Why aren't you in school? What happened?" I would respond, "Oh, I'm great. I'm this, oh,

I'm that," but deep down, I felt like a failure. It felt like people thought I had failed. Even though I knew I was returning to school in the winter, I still felt like I had failed to earn a scholarship. So I had to remain focused and stay committed to working out because my ultimate goal was to make it to the NFL.

I've never talked about it before. One of the biggest challenges I faced was being home with my dad and watching college football, seeing my former teammates play the following year. I felt like I had failed my father. Even though I knew I was returning to school, I felt like a failure. I didn't feel like a top-100 player from Texas. I felt like a bum, to be honest. Knowing that I had turned down over twenty scholarship offers and was now sitting at home was tough. I had been too focused on other people's journeys and didn't understand what was in store for me.

When I returned to Kansas State University, Coach Bill Snyder's son, Sean Snyder, spoke to me during our first practice. He said, "Mike, take the information that the person is saying, don't look at their skin color, but just take it and see how that works for you." It was like a blindfold had been lifted when

he told me that. Of course, it took some time to put it into practice since I had been raised a certain way for eighteen years. However, when I started looking at things from that perspective, I didn't care about someone's race or ethnicity. As long as they respectfully led me, I could work with them.

Adopting that mindset opened up doors for me. I played during my freshman and sophomore years, and although I was included in many different packages, I didn't have a starting role. Nevertheless, I was determined to start, thinking, "We're playing college ball to make it to the NFL." When I first arrived on campus, my coach, Mike Smitty, sat me down with my parents and said, "Mike, I'm looking you in the eyes. You're coming to school to play football, get your degree, and make it to the NFL. We're going to help you do that." I focused on that goal and graduated with my degree in two years while playing college football.

When it was time for me to graduate, I didn't even realize it was coming up in my junior year. I was sitting with my academic advisor when she asked me if I was ready to apply for graduation. Surprised, I replied, "I still have two years left on the field. What do you mean?"

She told me I had been taking 12 to 21-hour course loads each semester without realizing it. I was taking intersession classes, which were full course loads completed in only four weeks. These sessions took place right after the winter break and from May to June, which were known as summer sessions. I couldn't take intersession classes between session classes, so I took the May intersession classes because they paid us

$750 to take the class. As a broke college student, I couldn't resist the opportunity to make some extra money. Since we didn't have the NIL or living stipend then, the $750 was a huge help.

Thanks to these classes, I was able to graduate within two years. However, it worked out because my senior year in the classroom was equivalent to my junior year on the field. I had grayshirted, which meant I still had a redshirt and three years of eligibility left on the field.

And so coming into my junior year, I was getting ready to start. This was my time; I worked my butt off. It was my time to shine. But that was a hard summer. I had been falling out of workouts; I had full-body cramps, and we did not understand what was happening. My coach was thinking, *Mike is out drinking and partying, and now he's having full-body cramps.* The workout reports from my strength and conditioning coach revealed I wasn't finishing workouts. They just thought, *Man, this dude doesn't care; we're not going to play him.*

After that first game, I was still battling for the Mike linebacker position. I started in the Sam linebacker position and was in the defensive impact on a passer specialist. So, I had a lot of jobs, but I wanted that main Mike linebacker job. One of the things that my dad and coaches always taught me was, "You are not going to get to the NFL if you're not on the field, and you're not going to get to the NFL if you're not that guy who's able to take over games." So, I knew I had to play. We played against Stephen F. Austin that junior year and had a great game. I did really well, but I was still battling for the Mike line-backer position.

After the game, I urinated blood that Sunday, but I didn't tell anybody. I was fighting for a starting position and trying to make it to the league. The next time I went to the bathroom, there was still some blood, but I thought I was getting better, so I didn't say anything to my trainers. After that, we had practice, and that Tuesday, we had a brutal practice. I managed to finish the practice, but when I got home and tried to cook dinner for my pregnant wife, I couldn't stand up because of the excruciating back pain. Despite my wife urging me to go to the hospital, I was hesitant because of my dedication to the game.

My dad always said, "There is a difference between pain and injury. You can manage a little pain, but if you're injured, that's understandable." I figured, "I have workouts in the morning; I'll just talk to my trainers." I'm grateful for my wife because she insisted and told me that if I didn't go, she would call someone who would make me go.

My parents advised me to call my trainer, so I did. The trainers were surprised that I didn't tell them earlier and instructed me to meet them at the hospital. We arrived at the hospital, where they admitted me and started taking my vitals. The doctors discovered that my creatinine level was 3.5; if it reached level 5, my kidneys would explode, putting my life in danger. My body was going through rhabdomyolysis, but they still didn't know what was happening then. My body was shutting down, so their main focus was to lower my creatinine level and take care of my kidney function.

I was determined to get out of the hospital and back to it. Although my creatinine levels returned to normal after a week, I still struggled with nausea, dizziness, blurry vision, and the inability to keep anything down. Top of FormAfter being released from the hospital, I tried to return to practice that upcoming week, but it wasn't going well.

And so, my doctor ordered me to get blood drawn every day for two weeks. Every day, I had to go down to get my blood drawn so they could look at my levels. However, the results were still unclear. Finally, my mom suggested, "Okay, let's order a CAT scan and a full-body MRI to see what's going on." I will never forget that Sunday when my team had practice and wanted me to come up so I could be a part of the film session. My trainers had just received my results and said, "Hey Mike, we got your results back. Come see us, and then you can go in and watch the film."

The same day, we had my first son's baby shower. I remember it like it was yesterday. I'll never forget it. First, I talked to my wife and told her that I was headed up to the facility to get my results. Then, my mom and my dad were going down to Kansas City, where my wife is from, and we were going to do our baby shower. My team was out on the field when I arrived. However, none of the doors were open, so I asked someone to let me in. I entered the training room and saw Coach Snyder talking to the team as they were wrapping up practice and about to come in to shower.

Matt came in, hugged me, hugged my mom, and sat down. He had a look on his face, but I thought that they had a hard practice and something had happened to him during practice. Then, he said, "Mike, we got your results back, and you have a pituitary tumor." I was like, "All right, what does that mean? When can I get back to ball?"

He said, "No, I don't think you understand. You have a brain tumor. There's no playing ball. You cannot play ball with a brain tumor. We know you graduated, and this is your last semester of school, so we will allow you to finish the rest of your scholarship. You'll be a part of the team, but football is out of the question right now."

At that time, my whole world was crushed because I had been planning to make it to the NFL my entire life. And at this point, I was told that was not an option. I never thought about doing anything else outside of football. That was the first time I heard, "Mike, it's time to start thinking about things outside the game." I didn't understand what that meant. They sent me to an endocrinologist in Topeka, Kansas, Dr. Charyse Sindler. I love her. I went down there and started to get on treatment, trying to see how we could remove this tumor. Football was out of the question. I wouldn't practice or do anything like that because they needed me to get healthy. However, I was going to class to finish out my scholarship.

During a meeting with Dr. Sindler, she reviewed my charts and questioned whether my son was truly mine. She was amazed that I could do so much because my body was operating like that of a 77-year-old man with a testosterone level at that same age. She pointed out that with such low levels, I should not have been able to produce children. I assured her my son was mine and had him tested to prove it.

Dr. Sindler prescribed medication to shrink my tumor but warned me to take it carefully. I was not to take it before or after the scheduled time, and missing a dose could be risky. While the medicine was expected to shrink the tumor, it could also harden my heart, potentially causing a heart condition. So, we set a timeline from September to March for the treatment plan. So, I get on the medicine, and I start working out. I'm bigger, faster, stronger. I think my tumor has shrunk because I'm measuring off all the charts, and I'm back as captain. And they're just blown away. We are getting ready for spring ball and about to start practicing.

My follow-up appointment arrived, and the doctor conducted a CAT scan and the necessary tests. Unfortunately, the results showed that my tumor had grown and not shrunk as expected. I asked if I could get back to playing football, feeling as great as I was, but she informed me that playing football with a tumor in my brain was not an option and that the tumor had started to press down on my optic nerve, causing blurry vision and the need for glasses. However, she was concerned and told me she would send my case to her colleagues to determine the best course of action.

Eight of nine doctors said I'd never play football again. They would have to crack open my skull, pull my whole pituitary gland out, and I'd be on medicine for the rest of my life. They said there was no way that I would be a Division 1 athlete on top of that being able to produce a kid and that I shouldn't be playing football. There was one doctor that said he could do experimental surgery down at the National Institution of Health, but I had to get accepted into the hospital because it's a government-facilitated hospital. So, they would do the brain surgery there, but I had to get accepted by the endocrinologist for my kidney specialist.

After examining my case, they couldn't believe it, and I was accepted into the National Institutes of Health in Bethesda, Maryland. They flew me down there for the surgery, which at the time was experimental, though I've heard it's more common now. First, the surgeons made incisions under my lip and broke my nose, moving it to the side. They then removed my tumor piece by piece by accessing my brain through my nasal canal.

They inserted a breathing tube into my mouth during the surgery, but it was the wrong size, so they had to remove it. Unfortunately, when they removed it, they accidentally cut my throat, which resulted in blood coming out after the surgery. To stop the blood from filling my mouth, they had to use a suction every five minutes, and I had two long things coming out of my nose, making it difficult to breathe through my broken nose. I was given an oxygen mask, and the only way I could receive oxygen was through my mouth while they suctioned blood out of my throat.

After the surgery, I spent three days in recovery before flying back home to Dallas. I was on bed rest for six weeks and couldn't pick up anything over ten pounds. Later, I went back to Bethesda for a follow-up, and all my test results came back clear. My vision had improved, and my testosterone level had reverted to a thirteen-year-old boy's. The doctors told me not to be surprised if my wife was pregnant again when I returned home. As it turned out, my wife was indeed pregnant again when we returned.

So now I'm feeling great, but I need to build my body back up. I returned to Manhattan,

Kansas, in June to prepare to play ball again. When I arrived at Kansas State University, I couldn't walk fifty yards or jog twenty. I almost passed out during my first walk around the field. I knew I had to take things slowly, so I started walking and jogging. For two months, I focused on these exercises. By August, I was back to starting and stronger and faster than before. I played again in the upcoming season. So, I had the surgery in April, went back to school in June, and was playing again that August. However, in September, I was dealt another blow; my father passed away suddenly from a heart attack.

And now I'm faced with a dilemma because I've already graduated. I can be a graduate transfer, return to SMU, the school that wanted me before I left, and be by my family to run the family business and finish playing ball. At that time, I wasn't playing much at Kansas State University, not knowing they were easing me into the game after my brain surgery. I was ready to be playing right away. Once I came back to Kansas State after burying my father, we played against TCU. They didn't let me play but geared me up for the next week. After that game, we played Texas, and I played as Mike linebacker. From that game on, I started playing a lot.

Before returning to Kansas, my wife and mom asked if I wanted to play football. I told them no. I wanted to be by my family and didn't want to go back. My mom reminded me that I wasn't raised to quit. So I decided to finish the season, and then we would figure out what to do next. That was the best decision ever. I came back and had seventy-five tackles within the next seven games. I was a defensive player in our bowl game and helped our team go to a bowl game by defeating West Virginia with seventeen tackles, and it was just crazy.

It never would have happened if I had given up. I had a great season the following year, and we were getting ready for the draft. During that time, I went through a divorce finalized three days before the draft. Unfortunately, my name wasn't called in the draft. So many teams told me I was on their draft board. I even got three calls on the draft day with people telling me I was on their draft board, but I never got one. Finally, my agent called me and said, "Hey, I don't know why you didn't get drafted, but the good thing about this is you can choose where you want to go."

This is something I want to share with everyone who is trying to get drafted. How the draft works is that the players who are picked between the first and fourth rounds are the ones that teams have invested in the most. Those players pretty much have a set job for the upcoming year. On the other hand, the individuals drafted from the fifth to the seventh round are more like priority free agents. The team has invested less in them and can be cut if they don't perform well.

The downside of getting drafted in the fifth through seventh rounds is that I don't get to choose which team I go to. However, as a free agent, I had the opportunity to select the team that was the best fit for me. As a priority free agent, I had the chance to choose a team that would best fit me. Unlike players drafted between the fifth and seventh rounds, I was free to choose the team that gave me the best opportunity to make the team and secure a job. My agent and I reviewed rosters and spoke to players on these teams to assess the opportunity. Making the team was critical, as that was the only way to get paid.

To increase my chances of securing a team spot, I contacted Tyler Lockett in Seattle to ask about their linebacker situation. Unfortunately, Tyler informed me that while he would love for me to join the team, their linebacker room was already full with four veteran linebackers and Arthur Brown, who had just graduated from Kansas State. Therefore, I was unlikely to beat out all those individuals for a spot on the team. Despite this setback, I continued to explore my options and eventually signed with the Los Angeles Chargers as a priority free agent.

What separated me from being a regular free agent was the $10,000 signing bonus they offered me. However, I still had to fight for a job and understand a little bit about the business side of things. It's not just about talent and caliber; it's about how the numbers align and what's happening in the back office with the GMs. This was the right move for me, as I played for them for four seasons and had a successful NFL career.

I had a great opportunity playing with the Chargers. I deeply admire Coach Anthony Lynn, Coach Mike Smith, and all of my coaches because they saw my talent and were invested in me as much as I was invested in them. They taught me how to handle the business side of things as well. Unfortunately, while with the Chargers, I had to have back surgery because I began experiencing paralysis in my left leg. It's crazy to think that I injured my hip flexor, and overcompensating for it caused me to blow out my back.

One of the key things we learned in training camp was that our performance was critical for securing a job. Any video footage of our games and practices was our resume, not just for our current team but all thirty-two teams in the league. We must give our all and put in maximum effort every time we played or practiced because we auditioned for potential future employers.

That made sense to me, so I was working hard even though I was experiencing pain. But overcompensating for a hip flexor injury led to a back injury that caused me to go paralyzed in my left leg. The coaches recommended surgery, and I was placed on injured reserve. However, unlike many other players in a similar situation, the Chargers kept me in Los Angeles and asked me to become a coach. Anthony Lynn said, "Hey, you become a coach. I want you in the practices and coming up here and training. I need you to invest in the team because we are counting on you next year."

During this time, I saw firsthand how every Tuesday, the team would invite seven to nine players to try out for our jobs. I realized that if the team had a shortage of players on one side of the ball, they would cut players from the other side to balance things out. Unfortunately, this happened to one of my close friends, who was cut despite being a talented defensive player.

So, I rented an apartment and stayed there the whole time. I witnessed how seven to nine players would come in every Tuesday to work out for our jobs. If someone went down on offense and we were heavy on defense, they would cut a defensive player, as happened to my close friend, who was the last man on our linebacker roster. They needed his space, so they cut him.

When a player gets cut, they get placed on the contract reserve, where any other team can buy their contract within forty-eight hours. My friend was on the injured reserve list when he got cut. He was sitting there for an hour waiting for his forty-eight-hour span to end when his agent called and said, "Hey, you cannot sign that contract; the Giants just picked up your contract. We're about to ship you out there. You're on the last flight today, so pack up your stuff." It was crazy.

I didn't understand then that this happens in the NFL. The roster is set, and the head coach doesn't have the power. The GM has the power. The GM is the money man who controls the players, deciding who stays and who goes. So while the head coach can suggest who they want to keep, the GM has the most power.

At the end of that season, I was feeling better. I wasn't 100% better, but in my mind, I had adopted the idea that I would die on the field. I was divorced from my wife. I was suffering. Even though I was in the NFL, I was hurting. I was meeting with a counselor four days a week. On the outside, everything looked great, but I was dying internally. I was determined to die on the field because that was where I was connected with my father.

Of course, that didn't happen, and as I look back on my experience in the NFL, I realize that it has prepared me for what I'm doing now. It has given me a sense of purpose and showed me why I am called to do what I'm doing. All the challenges and obstacles I overcame during that time have equipped

me for this moment. Now, I can share my story, inspire others, and let them know they can achieve anything. It just takes faith, patience, resources, and an understanding of the system in which you want to get involved. It will take time and hard work, but it's possible.

Football was thrown upon me, and I didn't have a choice. I want to leave you with a couple of things today. Firstly, for the fathers. My father was a great man, and I loved him dearly. He lived his dream through me, and when I finished playing football, I went into a deep depression. I felt lost and didn't know who Charmeachealle was, my purpose, or which direction to go in. I wasn't worried about getting a job. That wasn't the problem. Internally, I had pushed so much trauma aside that when football was removed, everything came back all at once. I had to face it and get to the root of what was causing my mental blockers.

After doing so, I was able to see life much clearer. I stopped hating people and life because I felt abandoned. I felt like I was sold a dream and lied to my whole life. But, in the end, nobody lied to me. I just wasn't given the whole truth.

I wouldn't change anything for the world. I genuinely believe in knowing the ins and outs before jumping into something. If more players understood that the NFL stands for Not For Long, they would better equip themselves. They should see that only the Tom Bradys, Ray Lewises, and Ed Reeds of the league have five-plus-year careers, while the average player's lifespan is only two to three years.

After reaching your goal, what's the next chapter in your life? As a youngster, I heard people say, "What's your plan B?" I hate that question. I responded, "I don't have a plan B because I won't fail." Instead, ask, "What will you do after football?" The latter question reframes the conversation on a transition into something else.

If you are talking to student-athletes with dreams of making it into professional sports, it's essential to ask, "What will you do once you're done with this, even when you make it to the professional realm?" Because you'll make it, but that will end one day."

My transition into post-football life led me to build a system to help other players transition. Then, when I went into the school system, I saw an opportunity to use our influence to build up the school system and the students and their parents. While many nonprofits and individuals focus on building up the kids, I also saw the need to work with parents. Our babies, as I call them, are already behind due to the pandemic, and they're trying to pick up from where their world stopped.

The pandemic was a significant disruption for everyone, especially our kids. Everything they had been told about the world was questioned, and they saw their role models and adults struggling to survive. These kids are still in limbo, trying to figure out what's real and what's not. Many of their parents are also in limbo, trying to provide and take care of their families, which can be overwhelming. We need to provide job opportunities and support for these parents so that we can change the schools and the community and each household.

Our nonprofit, We L;ving, was started in 2021, and we also have a for-profit business, Pro Living. That's what we do. We're helping individuals live life, not just exist through it. After retiring from football, I was just existing, letting the day control me instead of taking control of the day. But now, I no longer carry that failure mentality where I look at my situation and feel inadequate. I'm using my story to empower others and to help them understand that there's a lot of work to be done. You can't just wake up and let life carry us out. You have to choose to live life every day.

7 STEPS TO CREATING A STRONG BRAND IDENTITY

In the crowded, competitive landscape of the modern economy, a strong brand identity can be the compass that sets your business apart from the crowd. Your brand identity is more than a logo or catchy tagline: it embodies your company's core values, aspirations, and personality. It's the essence of who you're as a company and how your customers perceive you. So how can you develop a strong brand identity? Let's dive deeper.

Understand the core of your brand

The path to a strong brand identity starts with understanding your brand's core. To do this, you need to define the key elements that set your company apart: your mission, your vision, your values, and your unique selling proposition (USP).

Your mission is what your company wants to achieve, the purpose that drives your actions. Your vision is the future you aspire to, the ultimate goal you want to achieve. Your values are the guiding principles of your business, and your unique selling proposition sets you apart from your competitors.

These elements form the foundation of your brand identity. They should be the North Star that guides your decision-making process and influences everything from product development to your marketing strategy to customer service. Therefore, the first step to a strong brand identity is clearly and compellingly defining these elements.

Identify your target audience

A compelling brand identity resonates with your target audience. That's why it's essential to know who your target audience is. What are their demographic characteristics, such as age, gender, location, and income level? What are their interests, needs, and wants? What problems do they have that your product or service can solve?

The more accurately you determine your target audience, the more effectively you can develop a brand identity that appeals to them. This includes creating customer personas—detailed representations of your ideal customers—to help you make brand decisions.

Designing your brand elements

After you've defined your brand's core and identified your target audience, the next step is to design the visual elements that will represent your brand identity. This includes your logo, color scheme, typography, and other visual elements symbolizing your brand.

Your logo is often the first touchpoint between your brand and potential customers; therefore, it should be memorable and reflect your brand personality. Your chosen color scheme and typography should match your brand personality and visually appeal to your target audience.

Create a brand voice

Your brand voice—the tone and style of your communications—is another critical component of your brand identity. It should reflect your brand personality and resonate with your target audience.

Your brand voice can be friendly, professional, playful, or authoritative. Whatever tone you choose should be consistent across all communication channels and platforms, from your website and social media to your email marketing and customer service.

Develop a brand story

Humans are naturally receptive to stories. We feel connected to and can relate to and remember them. Your brand story is a narrative about your company that summarizes your mission, values, and unique selling proposition in a way that appeals to your audience.

A compelling brand story can evoke emotion, drive loyalty, and set your brand apart. It's a powerful tool that, when used properly, can become a key differentiator for your brand.

Consistency is the key

Consistency is the golden rule when it comes to brand identity. It ensures that your brand is instantly recognizable and memorable. From the logo and color scheme to the language and messaging of your brand, every aspect of your brand identity should be consistent across all touch points. This consistency reinforces your brand identity and helps build trust with your customers.

Evolve with your audience

Consistency is important, but it's equally important that your brand identity evolves in line with your audience and market trends. As the market landscape changes over time, so should your brand identity. By regularly reviewing your brand identity, you can ensure that it stays relevant and resonates well.

Developing a robust brand identity is both a strategic and creative process. It requires a deep understanding of your brand's core, target audience, and market dynamics. Then, with a clear mission, a well-defined target audience, compelling visuals, a consistent brand voice, and a compelling brand story, you can create a brand identity that stands out from the crowd and resonates well with your target audience.

The path to a strong brand identity is an ongoing process that requires constant refinement and development. However, with careful planning, strategic thinking, and a customer-centric approach, your brand can develop a unique identity that reflects the essence of your business and leaves a lasting impression on your customers.

AN AUTHORITATIVE GUIDE ON HANDLING CONFLICT

In the dynamic world of business, it's not uncommon for the calm seas of smooth cooperation to be disturbed by the turbulent waves of conflict. Different perspectives, values, strategies, or interests can lead to disagreements and create a challenging working environment. However, when skillfully addressed, these conflicts can be transformed into valuable opportunities for growth, innovation, and strengthened interpersonal relationships. This comprehensive and detailed guide offers sound insights into effectively managing and resolving conflict, transforming potential obstacles into stepping stones on the path to success.

Understand the nature of conflict

The first step to effective conflict management is understanding the nature and origin of conflict. Conflict arises from disagreements or disputes over ideas, perspectives, interests, or goals. For example, conflict can be triggered in an organization by misunderstandings, unclear roles or expectations, competition for limited resources, or differences in personal styles or values. When leaders recognize and understand these dynamics, they can develop appropriate strategies to address conflict and prevent it from escalating, creating a more harmonious and productive work environment.

Recognize the conflict and own up to it

Avoidance or denial are common responses to conflict, but they often worsen the problem instead of solving it. The first step in dealing with conflict is to acknowledge its existence openly. This requires identifying the causes of the conflict, the parties involved, and the underlying issues that led to the disagreement. By recognizing and understanding the conflict, you lay the groundwork for resolution and equip yourself to approach the situation with objectivity, insight, and clarity.

Facilitate open communication

After recognizing and acknowledging the conflict, the next important step is to facilitate open communication. This includes encouraging all parties involved in the conflict to express their views, feelings, and concerns openly, honestly, and respectfully. Open dialog closes gaps in understanding, eliminates misunderstandings (often the root cause of conflict), and fosters a shared understanding of the situation. As a leader, creating a safe and supportive space where everyone's voice is heard and valued to resolve conflict effectively is essential.

Active listening—a critical skill for conflict resolution

Listening is an important but often under-appreciated skill in conflict resolution. However, active listening goes beyond just listening. It means giving the other person undivided attention, showing empathy, and validating their feelings and perspectives. This approach builds mutual trust and understanding and shows that you respect the other person's point of view and value their input. It's an important tool to promote effective communication and facilitate conflict resolution.

Strive for win-win solutions

Effective conflict resolution isn't about one party winning and the other losing. Nor is it just about compromise, where each party gives up something to find middle ground. Instead, it's about finding win-win solutions that meet the needs and concerns of all parties involved. This approach fosters mutual goodwill and strengthens relationships because everyone considers and respects their interests. Achieving win-win solutions requires creativity, flexibility, and negotiation skills to find solutions that meet the

various interests and achieve the best possible outcome for all parties involved.

Using mediation as a lever

In certain situations, conflicts can escalate to the point where they can no longer be resolved through direct communication alone. In such cases, mediation can be a valuable tool. A neutral third party can provide an objective perspective, facilitate communication, and guide the conflicting parties toward a mutually acceptable solution. In addition, mediators can help clarify issues, promote understanding, and propose fair and equitable solutions to build a bridge to resolution and reconciliation.

Learning from experience

Regardless of its nature or outcome, every conflict is an invaluable opportunity to learn and grow. By reflecting on the conflict and its resolution, you can learn lessons to improve your understanding and handling of future conflicts. Think about what led to the conflict, how it was managed, what worked and what didn't, and how you can avoid or better manage similar situations in the future. This reflective learning can foster personal growth, improve conflict resolution skills, and contribute to professional development.

Foster a positive work environment

Creating a positive, inclusive, and respectful work environment is beneficial to minimize conflict and its potential adverse effects. This includes fostering open

communication, mutual respect, and collaboration among team members. It's also essential to set clear expectations, define roles and responsibilities, and foster a culture of appreciation and recognition. Such a work environment can prevent conflict from arising, boost morale, increase productivity, and contribute to the company's overall success.

While conflict is inevitable in any business environment, it need not be viewed as exclusively negative. Instead, they can catalyze growth, innovation, and better relationships when managed and overcome effectively. By understanding the nature of conflict, acknowledging it, promoting open communication, actively listening, seeking win-win solutions, mediating when necessary, learning from experience, and fostering a positive work environment, you can transform conflict from a potential obstacle into a powerful catalyst for positive change. Remember, not the absence of conflict makes a successful team or organization, but the ability to resolve it effectively, learn from the experience, and grow stronger together. No matter the size of the conflict, the right approach can lead to greater understanding, collaboration, and shared success.

HOW TO MOTIVATE AND INSPIRE YOUR TEAM TO ACHIEVE GREATNESS

In the dynamic world of business, a motivated and inspired team is the engine of success. Building such a team, however, is no small feat. It requires leadership skills, people skills, empathy, and a commitment to fostering a culture of growth and innovation. So how does a leader cultivate this environment?

Build a culture of trust

Trust is the cornerstone of any successful relationship. It's the difference between a team that just functions and one that thrives. As a leader, it is essential to create an environment where employees feel safe to voice their ideas, concerns, and even their failures.

This starts with transparency. Be open about your decision-making process. Explain the rationale behind your decisions and ask for feedback. Show your team that you value their opinion.

But transparency alone isn't enough. You must also show humility and vulnerability.

Admit when you're wrong, and don't be afraid to be open about your mistakes. This fosters a non-punitive culture where employees feel comfortable taking risks, which in turn is a catalyst for innovation.

Set clear goals

The power of clear and meaningful goals cannot be underestimated. Employees who know the overarching goals of their work are more likely to feel motivated and committed to their company's goals.

As a leader, you have a responsibility to provide this clarity. Paint a vivid picture of the company's vision and explain how each task contributes to that overarching goal. This increases productivity and creates a sense of purpose and belonging among your team members.

Recognize and reward accomplishments

Recognition is a powerful motivator. When employees feel valued and seen, they're more likely to go above and beyond in their tasks. Recognition is more than just bonuses or public commendations, however.

Sometimes the most effective recognition comes in the form of a simple word of appreciation. A simple 'thank you' can mean a lot to an employee who has worked many hours on a project. The key is to create a culture where successes, big and small, are celebrated. This boosts morale and fosters a sense of camaraderie and team spirit.

Offer opportunities for advancement

Employees are motivated not only by their current tasks but also by what lies ahead. When you give them the opportunity to grow and develop, you show that you see and value their potential.

Offer professional development programs, mentoring programs, or challenging assignments that expand their skills. Encourage them to step out of their comfort zone. When employees see a clear path to advancement within the company, they're more likely to invest in their work and be motivated.

Encourage independence

Ownership is an important motivator. Conversely, micromanagement is one of the quickest ways to lower motivation. Giving your team the freedom to make decisions and solve problems independently can significantly boost morale and productivity.

This doesn't mean you leave them to their own devices. Instead, it means you give them the guidance and support they need while allowing them the freedom to take charge of their own work. This fosters not only creativity but also a sense of responsibility and accountability.

Lead by example

Leadership is as much about showing as it's about telling. Your team sees you as a role model. Your attitude, work ethic, and behavior set the tone for your team.

Show enthusiasm for your work. Maintain a positive attitude even when you face challenges. Show that you're resilient and have a strong work ethic. As a result, your team will likely follow your lead, creating a ripple effect of motivation and inspiration.

There is no magic formula for motivating and inspiring your team. First, it requires a deep understanding of your team members, including their motivations and goals. It takes an environment that values open communication, recognizes effort, and provides opportunities for growth. Finally, it takes a leadership style that exemplifies the values you want for your team.

This task may seem daunting, but it's important to remember that motivation isn't a destination - it's a journey. It's not about quick fixes or grand gestures; it's about creating an environment where motivation can thrive. It's about always being there for your team, supporting them, giving feedback, and recognizing their accomplishments.

It's also about understanding that motivation isn't a one-way street. As a leader, you also need to stay motivated and inspired. That means taking care of your mental and physical health, constantly learning and developing, and getting feedback from your team. After all, a motivated leader is a pre-requisite for a motivated team.

To effectively motivate your team, you must recognize that each individual has their own goals and desires. Then, adjust your approach to address individual needs while pursuing a collective vision for the team. This balance between personal recognition and collaborative goal setting can spur your team to new heights of performance.

Encouraging autonomy is another vital aspect. Allow your team members to take responsibility for their tasks and make decisions. This doesn't mean you abandon them. Instead, give them guidance and support when needed, but resist the urge to micromanage. This fosters a sense of responsibility and can significantly increase morale and productivity.

In summary, creating a motivated and inspired team is both an art and a science. It requires empathy, patience, and a willingness to adapt. It's not always easy, but the rewards—a motivated, engaged, and loyal team—are undoubtedly worth the effort.

Remember, as a leader, you can ignite the flame of motivation and inspiration in your team, creating a ripple effect that fosters success.

DOING GOOD IS
GOOD BUSINESS

SHARING THE CREDIT

Your business can give to charity without writing a check. Visit **www.SharingTheCredit.com** and start giving today.

www.ingramcontent.com/pod-product-compliance
Lightning Source LLC
Chambersburg PA
CBHW042009080426
42734CB00002B/28